ASKING FOR MONEY

**The Entrepreneur's Guide
to the Financing Process**

G. Bradley Mathewson

FSA

Financial Systems Associates, Inc.
Orlando, Florida

Published by Financial Systems Associates, Inc.

Library of Congress Catalog Card Number 89-80878
ISBN 0-9623770-0-7

Printed in the United States of America
Published August, 1989

for Christopher

CONTENTS

FOREWORD

I first started to write this book in 1982. In the intervening years, I've taken it out and put it away twice. It is much more complicated (and much more work) to write a book than I ever thought it would be. But the reasons I originally had for starting the book continue to exist. Every time I help someone prepare a financing proposal (or every time I have to tell someone that a project will not attract investors), I find myself telling them the same things. Every owner I work with seems to need the same information concerning financing proposals and the process of obtaining financing.

It occurred to me that if first-time entrepreneurs knew what happened when they asked for money and if they knew how to prepare a complete, well-written financing proposal, their chances of finding money would be significantly enhanced. If, in addition, they knew something about the people who are available to help them and something about some of the other less helpful people out there, they would be even better equipped to search for money.

This book is my response to those needs. It is not intended to be technical, although there is enough technical information in it to show you how to prepare a good financing proposal. It is intended to outline the whole process of asking for money, with some emphasis on the financing proposal itself, giving you forewarning of what you will go through and whom you will meet when you ask for money. None of the information presented here is unique or proprietary, but I haven't seen it readily available in one place until now.

We are all aware of the statistics concerning the failure rate of new businesses. Most failures occur in the first few years of operation and are a direct result of poor planning and/or inadequate research on the part of the owner. The wrong location; poor product selection; undercapitalization; lack of inventory control; accounts receivable problems; and the number one reason, inadequate sales volume. All these problems are the result of poor planning or inadequate research. Investors are aware of these statistics, also, and they look for proof that an entrepreneur has the skills and has done the homework necessary for success.

A properly prepared formal financing proposal demonstrates your management skills by providing evidence that you have examined each part of your project in detail, identified potential problems and developed strategies to minimize the effects of the problems. It proves to potential investors that you know your project. It shows how much money you need and how you plan for your project to pay for itself, operate at a profit and provide an adequate return to your investors within a reasonable amount of time.

If you follow all the procedures outlined here when you prepare your financing proposal, you will have looked at all aspects of your project and you will be much better equipped, not only to prepare a successful financing proposal, but also to operate your business successfully.

Brad Mathewson
August, 1989

SHOULD YOU ASK FOR MONEY?

Every person who owns a business—large or small, new or old—has had to ask for money at some point. Whenever a business is started, someone puts up enough cash to pay for the assets and operations of the business until it is able to generate sufficient cash on its own. Money must be obtained to purchase or expand an existing business, to begin a new product line, to move a business to a new location, or just to replace existing equipment. Money must also be obtained to start a new business. In this book, any such activity that has resulted in your need for money is referred to as a "project."

You are about to join the ranks of those who have asked for money. Your "project," whether it be a new business, an existing business, an expansion, a replacement, or something else, requires some amount of money in order to be realized. The fact that you are reading this means you do not have the necessary funds yourself. You are going to have to ask somebody for money.

SOURCES OF MONEY

The most common source of money for entrepreneurs is their own circle of insiders. Generally, this means your family: your mom, your dad, your rich wife, your Uncle Fred. This source of money is by far the easiest to tap. (After all, if your mother won't finance you, what makes you think that some prune-faced banker will?) In most cases, the amounts of money provided by a family are fairly small, mainly because small amounts are all that most families can afford. I realize that some families can put up substantial amounts of money, but, if your family is in that category, you do not need this book.

A more complete title to this chapter might be: "Should You Ask For Money from Outside Investors?" Obtaining money from parties unrelated to you is a complex and sometimes frustrating process. By the time you have finally obtained money from outside investors, you will have had to overcome your feelings of personal rejection resulting from the reactions of the majority of investors who either will not talk to you or who think your project is a foolish idea. You've also had to put aside any animosity resulting from their personal questions and their insinuations about your own finances and lifestyle.

We are going to describe the steps you must take when you ask for money in order to maximize your chances of being successful. Before we go over those steps, however, we are going to examine some of the many reasons entrepreneurs do not get the money they need, so that you will have a better idea of what to expect and perhaps whether your search for money has any hope of success.

OBSTACLES TO OBTAINING MONEY

The three primary reasons that entrepreneurs do not obtain money from outside investors are:

1. The necessary funds can be raised from within their own circle of insiders (family, close friends, etc.).

2. Outside investors refuse to provide the money.

3. Outside investors will provide the money, but want too much from the entrepreneur in return.

The harsh reality is that every investor is looking for a reason to refuse to provide money to you. The percentage of requests for money that are actually filled is fairly small. It really is a jungle out there. If you cannot get through this chapter with a smile on your face, there is no need for you to go further. You do not have the determination necessary to get money from outside investors.

Assume you are beginning your project. You have discussed it in general terms with some of your friends. Usually, there will be at least one person you know who will say, "There is more money than there are projects to invest in," or, "If you can come up with a good project, I can get you the money." Both of these statements are commonly made and often have some credence. Your acquaintance may have participated, at least peripherally, in obtaining financing for a project in the past, giving increased credibility to those statements.

Unfortunately, both of these statements will almost always be false when it comes to your project. There **is** more money than there are projects to invest in. But only for "safe" projects And you can be sure that your project will not be considered "safe" by your acquaintance's contacts. Therefore, almost certainly, when you bring your project to your acquaintance, there will not be any money for you from that quarter.

There are as many reasons why entrepreneurs do not find money as there are investors. In some instances, entrepreneurs do not find money because their project does not fit an investor's area of interest. Investors are looking for investments such as an Apple Computer or a Microsoft, where the return on their investment is thousands of times their initial investment.

In their search for these elusive "big hits," investors tend to "specialize" in certain fields, such as electronics or computers or communications. ("Specialize" is in quotes because, even though investors limit themselves to certain types of investments, they are by no means true specialists or experts, and rarely have any real knowledge of the industries in which they choose to invest.) However, whether or not investors know what they are doing, they do know what they want. They also know what they don't want.

Investors don't want to have to make any hard decisions about whether an individual investment is, in fact, a good business investment. Investors want to see the project's earnings history. They want to see a lot of assets and substantial cash flow. Investors want to feel that their investment is reasonably secure, even if they do not know anything about how the business actually operates. They want to see earnings projections and cash flow projections which predict a high return on their investment (usually 20% to 50% per year). Investors want to feel that even if the return on their money is lower than projected, they will not lose their money.

As you can imagine, looking at projects in this fashion will many times lead to bad investments, where the investor does, in fact, lose money. Much more frequently, however, it results in the situation where a project, which is in fact a good investment opportunity, is simply rejected or ignored. When an investor refuses to invest in a project, the only one hurt is the entrepreneur. Investors have many alternate uses for their money. They can afford to be choosy. No investor ever lost any sleep because he caused a loss to an entrepreneur.

Many times an investment is refused by an investor because it is outside the investor's "investment parameters." For example, it is impossible to find an institutional investor (i.e., banks, savings and loans, insurance companies, etc.) that will invest in any start-up company. Likewise, they will not invest in a restaurant, a retail store, or an entertainment project. There are some venture capital companies and stock brokerage houses which will look at such projects, but they are few and far between, and they usually require that the project be fairly large—over $1,000,000.

Sometimes an investor will offer to make an investment in a project, but only on terms that are so onerous that the entrepreneur should turn down the investor. Included in this category are the classic cases: where the investor wants to steal the company from the entrepreneur through impossible payback terms; where the investor wants to put up 20% of the money for 80% of the company; where the investor wants to get all the money back and still own a big part of the company; and all of the other legends.

We've all heard one or more of those "horror stories." Although most of them are apocryphal, all have some basis in fact. After all, from an investor's perspective, such behavior is merely "protecting my investment," or "meeting my R.O.I. objectives." The investor has the cash and, thus, the control of the process. The conditions leading to such "horror stories" often arise because entrepreneurs can be so anxious to get the cash necessary to get their project going that they will agree to almost any terms, even though they know the terms are impossible to meet, just to get underway. Therefore, it's possible you might even contribute to your own problems through this type of overenthusiasm, or through lack of advice or misplaced trust.

The hardest task in any financing deal is to be objective about the amount of control or ownership you are willing to trade for the amount of money to be invested. You should be prepared to trade a major portion of control or ownership for an investment and you have to be aware that you may even have to agree to conditions under which you can lose your company and, perhaps, lose your rights to start a new company in the same industry. Of course, there are many instances in which a trade of your majority interest for an investor's money is appropriate. Every offer of financing you receive must be examined in detail. None should be rejected out of hand.

The point of this is that you have your ideas of what you are willing to give up in the way of ownership or control and investors have their ideas of what they need. Very rarely is there initial agreement on the subject of ownership between entrepreneur and investor. In most cases an investor will want significantly more than you feel you should give. You should talk it over with your advisors. If your advisors agree with you, then you must refuse the investment. But you must realize that you may be turning down the only offer you will get.

Now that we've discussed the negative aspects, you need to remember that entrepreneurs **do** find money. Investments **are** made. Happy endings **do** occur. What we have shown is that investors have more reasons for not investing than for investing. Finding money for a project is difficult—if it was easy, everyone would do it. But it can be done.

THE "GREAT LEAP OF FAITH"

You want to ask for money, so you surely already have a project that needs money. It does not matter how your project originated. As an entrepreneur, you may be one of those inventive people who can think of and design new products, or you may be an analytical person who has seen the need for a product or service to fill a particular niche in a market, or you might already own a business and your project is the expansion of that business. From whatever source, you must have a project (and you must have a very high degree of confidence in its success) before you can think about asking an investor to give you any money.

In most cases, you are going to ask for money from

people who don't know you, and who, at least initially, do not want to give money to you. You have to convince them that you and your project should get money from them. The fact that you know your project will succeed will not convince an investor. Investors want objectivity. They want to see facts. You have to show them that you have documented the data they need to make their decision. This is not as easy as it sounds. There are obstacles to overcome. The major obstacle to providing objective facts is that your project has not yet begun operations. You are, in essence, predicting the future.

We all realize that the future cannot be predicted precisely, but there are techniques for projecting the future behavior of those different elements of your project that are necessary to its future success. Some of these techniques are better and produce more accurate results than others. Every element of your project has its own generally recognized indicators of future behavior. You will prepare and present to your investor a detailed examination of those indicators and the effect of each on your project. This presentation will help to weave a fabric of credibility around your projections that will work to convince an investor that your project is worthy of an investment.

Credibility is critical to your presentation. No matter how many facts you present, you are still predicting the future, and an investor has to make what a consultant friend of mine calls "The Great Leap of Faith" before you can have any money.

The concept of "The Great Leap of Faith" revolves around the basic condition that the future is inherently unpredictable. Your estimate of market growth is based on the best economic forecasts. Your estimate of market penetration is based on an analysis of competition and the comparative advantages of your project's products or services. Your estimate of costs is based on the prices of the goods and the wages for the services your project needs. Your projected results of operations are a combination of all of the above. They indicate that your project will operate at a significant profit and generate plenty of cash flow. But the investor still has to make that "leap" from present facts to future events. You and your financing proposal are the platform from which the investor makes the "leap." In this chapter we will discuss how to determine whether or not your project has the potential to persuade an investor to make the "leap of faith." The actual financing proposal itself—format, style, etc.—will be covered later.

THE FEASIBILITY STUDY

In order to determine whether or not your project can make the grade, you will need a "feasibility study." You can perform this study yourself or you can hire an outside consulting firm which specializes in such studies. A feasibility study is nothing more than an objective look at your project, its products or services, its market, the costs of operation, and, from all that, a projection of the potential sales and profits for your project based on the size of the market, the number and size of your competitors, and the room for market growth. The purpose of such projections is to objectively determine whether or not your project will work. You already know that your project will be one of those which will be successful, but you must be able to prove it to an investor.

The primary determinant of future success is projected sales volume. Sales are the lifeblood of every business. Sufficient sales volume will, with adequate management, always assure the success of a project. Conversely, without sufficient sales volume, your project will fail.

Therefore, if the sales volume predicted from your feasibility study is not sufficient for the success of your project, you must find another project. You gain nothing by altering the projections so that they seem to show potential profitability. If the sales are not really there, your project will fail. If you have accurately determined the facts, as we will discuss in a later chapter, and if those facts do not indicate adequate sales volume, nothing can save your project. Many times projects fail even when objectively determined sales projections indicate the potential to attain sufficient sales volume. So if your projections do not show sufficient sales volume, your project can not and will not be successful.

Once you have objectively determined that your project will generate sufficient sales volume, you will examine the costs and expenses involved in your project. Your feasibility study will include an analysis of the costs and expenses of similar businesses in the same industry, adjusting for any differences between your project and those existing businesses. Using this analysis, the costs and expenses for your project can be projected. By comparing those projected costs and expenses to the projected sales volume you determined earlier, you can calculate whether or not your project has the capability of generating sufficient profits. Remember, your project not only has to cover its own costs of operation, but also your salary and any interest and carrying charges on the loans you receive, while still providing a good return to your investor. So, if it cannot produce fairly generous profits, you cannot expect to succeed. In that event, you must either alter your project so that it will make money, or you must abandon it.

With your feasibility study in hand, showing that your project has the potential to make money, you can proceed to the next step in securing money for your project: determining your need for outside consultants.

USING CONSULTANTS

You've identified your project and determined that it has sufficient sales and profit potential to be worth pursuing. Now what? Chances are you have not been directly involved in raising money for a project. Chances are you do not know anyone who has actually been directly involved in raising money for a project.

You need help. This should not make you feel inadequate. After all, even businesses as large as General Motors use outside help when they look for money to fund an acquisition or a new project. The General Motors of the world have already identified the help they need—they go to big investment banking firms like Goldman Sachs. They also have the luxury of choosing between different sources of financing, many of which are not even options for you. But the principle is the same: they do not raise money without help.

If your project is fairly small, your use of outside assistance will be limited. You cannot afford to spend thousands of dollars on consultants for a project that might only need slightly more than that amount to be fully funded. In such cases, you may use your friends as consultants. Or, perhaps you can do the whole job yourself using this book.

But if you have even a mid-sized project, you will more than likely wind up using several consultants or experts. You may have a team of experts: accountants, lawyers, brokers, architects, engineers, etc. You must identify the type of experts you need, sort through them, and pick the ones that are the most suitable for your project. Note that I didn't say the most qualified, but the most suitable. Many times, the most qualified experts will be too costly, too haughty, or just not your type of person.

One rule of thumb you can use is that no matter what other qualifications they have, your consultants need to be excited about your project. If your project is merely a bunch of numbers and billable hours to them, you have the wrong advisors. There are plenty of people who will work **for** you; you need someone who will work **with** you—someone who will take some responsibility for the accuracy of your projections, someone who will help you work on the documentation, and, most importantly, someone you can get along with. You don't have to be bosom buddies, but different people interact differently with one another, and there is no sense paying for a person you can't stand to be around. Let that person go work for someone else.

You may have used an outside expert or consultant to prepare your original feasibility study. It is usually better to have an outside firm perform such studies. This is because outside firms not only appear more objective and independent to a potential investor, they actually are more objective and independent. They can look at your project without too great an inclination to force the numbers to work out favorably. (They still want your project to work out, since you will be happier about paying their bill if they give you a favorable study, but they are not as anxious as you are.)

Investors place great reliance on the objectivity of outside consultants. In fact, investors will **always** believe the word or opinions of an outside consultant over the word or opinions of the owner. So another reason for using outside experts is that, properly chosen, the outside firm you use can provide your project with additional credibility by the association with an established, reliable consulting firm. This will apply to every expert you hire. Try to pick consultants with good reputations.

CHOOSING AN ACCOUNTANT/FINANCIAL EXPERT

Before you begin the rest of your financing proposal you need a good set of financial projections, so your first outside consultant will probably be an accountant/financial expert. You may already have such expertise yourself or you may have an accountant on your staff. But, just as it is usually desirable to have an outside, independent entity prepare your feasibility study, it is similarly desirable to have an outside expert prepare your financial projections.

Qualified assistance in preparing your financing proposal is harder to find than you might think. Relatively few people, even long-time accountants and lawyers, are experienced with financing proposals. In fact, very few people see more than one or two financing proposals during their entire business careers. Of those few who do see several financing proposals, fewer still possess the creative skills necessary to prepare a financing package. There's a lot more to it than merely taking a bunch of numbers and putting them together into a financial projection. You must create an atmosphere of intelligence and credibility.

Why not use a public accountant? Everybody knows the Big Eight and their "little brothers." Unfortunately, the rules of the public accounting profession preclude public accountants from preparing "business plans" or "financial projections" for use by third parties such as banks or investors. Members of the public accounting profession have decided that they deal only with "facts," not projections. The only predictions of the future they are allowed to prepare are "forecasts." A "forecast," by definition, is "the single most likely set of financial results" which will occur, given the current conditions surrounding a project.

Obviously, there is a tremendous amount of research required to document and support "the single most likely set of financial results." This research is so extensive that it can raise the cost of preparation of a public accountant's "forecast" to as much as ten times the cost of the much simpler "projection" prepared by a qualified accountant/financial expert. And most investors do not necessarily feel that a "forecast" is truly a more reliable prediction of future events. They do not give substantially more credence to a public accountant's "forecast" than to a "projection," so long as the "projection" is prepared by a reputable expert. Using a public accounting firm to prepare your business plan then, would seem an excessive expense, unless your investor requires it for some reason. (This will happen, for example, if your financing is coming from a public offering of stock underwritten by a major stockbrokerage firm.)

So how do you find the right expert? You start by talking to people in the same industry as your project. They will give you leads to accountant/financial experts who are familiar with the industry. The best situation for you would be if a single accountant/financial expert were named by two or three different sources. Unfortunately, there are so many investors, so many deals, and so many accountant/financial experts, that it is most likely you will not hear any name more than once. You can look for a name you've heard of, a conveniently-located office, or use some other system for picking your candidates. Pick two or three and interview them. Check their references. Look at their past work. Ask about fees. At least one of them should "feel" better to you. Choose that one. If none stand out, start the process over.

Good accountant/financial consultants will question you just as thoroughly as an investor would. They will help you develop the documentation for the assumptions accompanying your projections. They will examine the methodology you used to develop your conclusions about your market and help you determine the adequacy and accuracy of those conclusions. They are also able to write an intelligent and readable project description and help with the other parts of your financing proposal. Good accountant/financial consultants are more than merely "numbers persons."

It is important that your financial consultant know your industry, because each industry has its own rules and conventions for financial statements and financial projections. (What are the normal financial relationships? Where can you find different types of supplies? How many employees are required? What facilities do you need? Etc.) They will know what information you need to give an investor, and they should be able to help you generate it.

The cost of a good accountant/financial consultant will be from $2,000 to $4,000 per week. It will take at least one week to prepare the financial projections, even if you already have all the data. Be prepared for at least two weeks of work. After preparing your financial projections, your consultant should be able to help in the other sections of your financing proposal. You may want to negotiate a long-term consulting rate, which can be significantly lower than the hourly or weekly rate.

The person who actually does the work is important. Your accountant/financial consultant may have a large firm and may assign your project to one of the least experienced employees. Employees are rarely as interested in their work as the owner, and they oftentimes do not have the experience to be able to help on the rest of your proposal. You want your work done by the owner. Don't settle for less.

Your financial projections are the heart of your financing proposal. The expert who prepares your financial projections may therefore be the most important expert you select. You need to be sure that your accountant/financial expert can do the right job for you. However, this expert will also probably be the least expensive of all the experts you hire, and the financial projections will be available for review by your other experts, so the risk is somewhat lower in the event that you hire the wrong person.

CHOOSING A LAWYER

After the accountant/financial expert, the most often used expert is a lawyer. The process of finding a lawyer will be approximately the same as that used to find your accountant/financial expert—referrals. The accountant/financial expert who helped you with your financial projections will probably know several lawyers who have done legal work for other projects. In addition, the same sources from which you got the name of your accountant/financial expert should also be able to name some lawyers. Again, pick the two or three with whom you feel the most comfortable. Check references. Check current and former clients. You need a competent lawyer, experienced in working with investors, familiar with projects like yours, who can get along and work well with both you and your other consultants.

One area of legal expertise you will definitely need is securities law. Your financing proposal is part of your search for money. You expect to sell or exchange some portion of the ownership of your project for money from an investor. That's basically what they do on the New York Stock Exchange, and if you are not careful, you'll find yourself subject to, or in violation of, the rules and regulations of The Securities and Exchange Commission regarding the sale of unregistered securities. A good securities lawyer can help you avoid this. And it should not be too expensive. An experienced securities lawyer will not need to spend a lot of time figuring out what you can say and what you cannot say to potential investors.

How can you know whether attorneys know what they're talking about? You can get an idea by the number of hours they propose to bill you. For instance, if all you want is a review of your financing proposal and advice on how to avoid conflicts with S.E.C. laws, a lawyer shouldn't have to spend more than a couple of hours. If you negotiate before-hand, you might not have to pay too much for such short review. Be sure you get some sort of letter showing that a lawyer did, in fact, review your proposal.

You need to be somewhat careful when using an attor-ney. Many of the best ones have billing rates well in excess of $200 per hour. At those rates, it's easy to have a legal bill in excess of $10,000 before you know it. (That's only a week at $250 per hour.) You literally cannot afford to get a lawyer too deeply involved in your financing proposal (unless you have some unique relationship with your attorney), but you do need your proposal and any contracts you may want to sign with consultants and others reviewed for legal compli-ance. You will also need a lawyer to handle your financing agreements.

In some cases, lawyers will do some or all of the work you need in exchange for some ownership in your project. This saves you from having to pay out cash, but your lawyer is now your partner and not your independent consultant. And you still must know that your lawyer is competent. Poor legal advice is never free. It will cost you much in the long run.

It is difficult to identify the good lawyers. You can't get referrals from other lawyers, because they want your work themselves, and as you will find, most of them are "experts" in just the field you need. Many times you can use your potential investors as a source for lawyers. Investors deal with lawyers frequently and they may be able to suggest one for you. A lawyer referred by an investor will probably have most of the expertise you need for your project.

You must be careful in your choice of lawyers. While it is true that any one of your consultants can act contrary to your best interests, your lawyers, by virtue of the types of tasks they perform, can cause the greatest amount of difficulty if they are not ethical or competent. An unethical or incompetent lawyer can cause you to sign documents that are not in your best interests and that can literally haunt you for years or even cause you to lose control of your project. And it is so hard to evaluate the work of a lawyer until it is too late.

Your lawyer, like all your consultants, must be independent of your other consultants, in order to help you get the variety of opinions that will help you to make informed decisions. The independence of your various consultants also works to keep you from inadvertently getting involved in a situation where your consultants collaborate with each other to move your project in a direction that benefits your consultants more than it benefits you or your project.

CHOOSING A "BROKER"

In your search for investors, you will almost certainly run into one or more "brokers." You may quite possibly use a "broker" on your project. A "broker" is a middleman who has, through past dealings with investors or lenders, established enough credibility with one or more of them to be able to present projects to them for funding. A good broker can show you how to package your proposal in the manner most attractive to investors. In the best case, a broker will be able to assure you that investors will, in fact, look at your project and give it serious consideration. But no broker can promise more than that.

The brokers we are discussing are not the business brokers who advertise in the classified section of the newspapers. Those business brokers sell small businesses, and they are usually real estate brokers first. Not that they're bad, but they are not going to have the type of contacts you will need.

You do not have to use a broker. You can go to your

public library and copy the published lists of venture capitalists, insurance companies, banks, etc. You can contact each and every investor listed. You might have success. It is done all the time. However, most investors or lenders are literally inundated with unsolicited proposals, and many have become so overwhelmed that they will not even look at a proposal that does not come from a source with which they are already familiar.

In addition, there are sources of money which are not found in the books. Individual investors, for instance, who may be known only to brokers, lawyers, and tax accountants. Therefore, in order to maximize your chances of actually getting money, you will probably use at least one "broker" in addition to whatever other methods you use to contact potential investors.

A good broker can be very useful to you. The broker you use should be a person who has actually presented financing proposals to investors and obtained financing. You will probably need more than one broker, because there are so many individuals and firms with money to invest, no one broker can know more than a few. In addition, even the best brokers can only work on a few deals in a year, and no broker can sell every deal he works on. If you choose to use brokers, therefore, you should use several brokers, each with different contacts, to work with you on selling your project to investors.

Brokers are unusual animals and some of their behavior patterns may seem strange to you. The only assets brokers have are their contacts in the investment community. They are deathly afraid that you or someone else will steal those contacts and obtain funding for your project, leaving them out of the deal.

Thus, when you deal with brokers, the first thing everyone of them will say to you is, "I need an exclusive." An "exclusive" gives that broker the sole authority to present

your project to investors, and any fee to be paid in the event
you obtain funding from any source will go to that broker,
even if your funding actually resulted from someone else's
efforts.

Brokers will tell you that "their" investors will not
consider your financing proposal unless they have "control"
of it. Brokers will tell you that they cannot afford to spend
a lot of time on a project that everybody else can also submit
to investors. They might tell you that they only need an
"exclusive" for 180 days. Or they might tell you they only
need an "exclusive" for 90 days. Brokers will tell you almost
anything to get an "exclusive" from you.

It is mostly B.S. Brokers do not really need an "exclusive." You should not sign an "exclusive" contract with a
broker (or with anyone else, for that matter). However,
brokers do need "protection" on potential investors to which
they furnish information on your project. "Protection"
means that if one of the investors to which a broker sends
information on your project subsequently provides funding
(within a certain time limit), that broker will receive the fee,
even if another broker also provides information to the same
investor. This is fair, with certain limiting conditions: the
broker must provide you with a list of the investors which are
receiving information; and there should be some evidence
that the broker already knows someone at those investors'
offices. You don't want to have to pay a fee merely because
a broker did a mass mailing of your proposal. You can do a
mass mailing yourself as we discussed above.

Brokers work on the "come." That means they do not
get paid unless and until they arrange funding for your
project under terms acceptable to you. Their fee will almost
always be based on the net amount of money obtained. A
good rule of thumb for the amount of the fee is something
called a "Lehman formula." (No one at Lehman Brothers
ever published any such formula, but it is a good benchmark,

so we have included it here.) The fee based on this "Lehman formula" is:

5% of the first million dollars raised;

4% of the second million dollars;

3% of the third million dollars;

2% of the fourth million dollars; and

1% of any amounts raised in excess of four million dollars.

The fee you negotiate with your brokers may vary somewhat, depending on the amount of money you want, the type of project you have, whether it is a start-up or not, whether you want debt or equity funding, etc. (For example, if you go to a stockbrokerage for a public offering, you will pay at least 10% of the amount raised, with a minimum offering of $2,000,000.)

A broker may ask for "expenses." You may or may not agree to this. Expenses usually refer to costs incurred on trips to see investors. It is not unusual to provide reimbursement for travel expenses, as long as you have approved them **in advance**.

Brokers will also probably try to get you to agree to give them "warrants" as part of the fee for their performance. They will usually want "only" 3% or 4% of your company. Warrants will give them the right to purchase ownership in your project at a very favorable price without any prior monetary investment. I would think twice before giving warrants to your brokers. Their monetary fee is usually substantial and should be adequate without warrants.

However, you might agree to give warrants to your brokers based on the length of time it takes to obtain funding and/or the cost of the funding. If your brokers save you interest costs or help you retain a higher-than-expected percentage of equity, it is not unreasonable to reward them, but only afterward and only based on some predetermined standard of performance on their part.

Finding funding for your project can be a lot like looking at the performance of the stock market. The theory of the stock market is that the underlying fundamentals of a particular company will determine the price of its stock in the market. But when you compare the price behavior of a company's stock to the actual earnings performance of that company, the stock price movement can look almost random.

Using a broker seems to have some of that same random behavior. A given broker might present a given project to a given investor on a given day and get financing for it, perhaps even without regard to any real potential for the project's success. Conversely, a particular broker who just successfully submitted a financing proposal to a particular investor for a project identical to yours might not be able to get that investor to even return a phone call.

You need to be sure that the brokers you use stay within their own areas of influence. Brokers just waste their time and your time by contacting investors they do not know well. Worse, one broker may interfere with the efforts of another broker who may already have good contacts with a particular investor, causing arguments about who gets the fee and, in the worst case, mucking up your financing.

There are other things to look out for when dealing with brokers. If a broker asks for a fee "up-front," or before anything has been done, do not use that broker. Reputable brokers do not ask for up-front fees. Reputable brokers will work with you to create a contract which outlines the type of financing they will try to arrange for you, and the fee you will pay them if they arrange it. The contract will include their "protection." This is acceptable and even desirable. You are interested in dealing honestly with honest people, even if you need an ironclad contract to do it.

Some of them, however, may try to include in their contract with you some wording to the effect that if they bring you funding that meets the criteria set forth in the contract (amount, payback terms, interest rate, equity percent, etc.), and you refuse the funding for any reason, you will still owe them their fee. That is nice for the broker, but not for you. Do not agree to any contract with that clause.

Your broker(s) will work as hard as they feel they have to, and will work harder to the extent that they feel your project can be funded. Usually, if funding is not obtained in the first 60 to 90 days, they will lose interest (after all, they are not getting paid), and you will need to begin dealing with new brokers.

OTHER CONSULTANTS

Depending on the size of your project, you may need the services of other types of consultants. There are things you should be aware of with most types of consultants. For example, you may use an architect. Architects will design whatever you tell them, but you have to work closely with them to keep what they design from being too costly. One reason for this is that most architects are concerned to one degree or another with making an artistic statement. (That's one of the reasons they chose architecture.) A second reason might be that architects get paid a percentage of the cost of the building. The more it costs, the higher their fees.

You, on the other hand, are primarily concerned that your building won't fall down and that it can be built at a reasonable cost. If you downplay the art somewhat, and substitute practicality, you can almost always build what you need at your budget figure. But, you must know what you want and you must work with your architects closely, so that you can see what is going on at all times in order to help them give you what you want.

The same is true to some extent for civil engineers. They deal every day with governmental inspectors and other officials, and the natural inclination of some of them is to try to preserve and enhance their relationships with those people. Sometimes they will tend to engineer your project so that it exceeds the legal requirements in order that it will be easily approved by the regulatory bodies. (And, again, their fee is based to some extent on the complexity of their design.)

What you may not know until too late, is that once a design is approved by those governmental bodies, it is very difficult to make changes if you decide that you are "over-engineered." You need to make sure the engineering plans are exactly what you want, and no more than you need, before they are submitted for approval.

Vigilance and close coordination are required in your dealings with all your consultants. You cannot give any outside person the freedom to reduce your options. Whether they mean it or not, whether you know it or not, consultants can seriously affect your ability to secure financing and/or bring your project in on budget, if their work is not exactly what it should be.

I don't want to appear to be picking on consultants, but what they do can drastically affect the costs of your project. Many times, simple changes can greatly reduce costs without sacrificing anything; it's just another way of doing the same thing. But you won't know that if you don't work closely with your consultants.

PUTTING IT ALL TOGETHER

As you hire more and more experts, you are going to have to decide how much control they should have over your project. That is a question without a definite answer—every situation is different. Your consultants will generally have more general knowledge and more specific knowledge than you do concerning the dynamics of your industry and your search for funding; they may even know more about your project than you do. (After all, you wouldn't have hired them if they didn't know something you didn't know.)

But it is still your project. In the final analysis, you have to make the decision. Most of the time, your experts and you will agree on the decision. However, if they suggest something that does not feel right to you, then you do not have to accept their advice. Your consultants get to go home after they help you. You get to stay and live with their work. It's your project and the final decision is yours. Obviously, you wouldn't arbitrarily ignore your consultants' advice. That could cost you dearly. But sometimes their advice may not agree with the way you see your project, and you have every right to act on your feelings.

All your experts will need to work together, but stay within their own areas. The way this usually sorts out is that your broker(s) will work with your accountant/financial expert to develop the financing proposal. Your lawyer will work on the contract between you and your broker(s), will review your financing proposal, and will work with the broker to make sure that any financing deal proposed is consistent with your wishes and does not include any hidden surprises. Your accountant/financial expert will prepare most of your financing proposal and will help you evaluate the efforts of your broker and your lawyer. You will be receiving inputs from all your experts, and will have to make the final decision on any transactions. Thus, you can see why it is critical that your experts work together, even though they are independent of one another. You need their independent ideas, but you do not need them carping and backstabbing each other.

Your team of outside consultants may be larger or smaller than outlined above, but you will need all the areas of expertise. Some of the functions may be combined in one consultant, or you may use more than one consultant in one or more areas. In any case, your team, once assembled, will help you decide whether your project is worth pursuing (an outside opinion can't hurt), how much money you should ask for, and whether to ask for debt or equity financing.

But first they'll help you with your proposal.

JUSTIFYING YOUR PROJECTIONS

The number one absolute drop-dead certainty in your search for outside investors for your project is that no investor will just give you money. Before any of them will invest with you or loan you money, they want to know that they will get their money back. And they want to know how long it will take for them to get their money back. Just because you know that your project will succeed does not mean that investors will feel that their money is safe in your hands. If you can't convince investors that their money is safe, they won't let you use their money. And, if you don't get their money, your don't get your project.

Investors want facts, not convictions. But the success of your project will occur in the future and you can't present an investor with facts about the future. But you can present an investor with accurate, documented projections, using assumptions for the future behavior of the different elements of operations of your project. Valid assumptions are based on current conditions, logically extrapolated into the future. Investors understand projections prepared in this manner and will accept them as long as there is factual backup for each assumption.

THE IMPORTANCE OF REALISTIC PROJECTIONS

Your financial projections are the backbone of the financing proposal for your project. The assumptions used must be correct and reasonable. The accuracy of the assumptions and facts used to support the financial projections truly makes or breaks your search for financing for your project. If your assumptions are too pessimistic, your financial projections will show a too low a return for investors, and you probably will not get financed.

If your assumptions are too optimistic, on the other hand, your financial projections will show a higher return to investors than your project can realize. You may receive financing, but your project will probably not be able to meet the projections. This will make your investors very unhappy. Such an event can cost you a lot of money and perhaps, depending on the terms of your financing agreement, control of your own project. In this chapter, we are going to discuss how you arrive at the conclusions used to make the basic assumptions supporting your financial projections, and what factors are used in each.

Before you can present your project to an investor, you must determine for yourself whether or not it can be successful. Sales are the key to success. Sufficient sales volume coupled with adequate management will overcome any problem. Insufficient sales volume means your project will die. It is as simple as that.

Assuming that your unit sales price exceeds your unit costs, so that you make a profit on each unit sold, there is no business problem that cannot be solved if your sales are high enough. Conversely, in the long run, there is no way that your costs can be cut far enough to keep your project profitable if your sales are too low. This is a basic law of business. **It is always true.**

You have already made a quick estimate of the sales potential for your project in your feasibility study discussed earlier. Now you are going to study the sales potential for your project in detail. Product by product. Service by service. Your feasibility study merely indicated that there was room in your industry for another competitor. You are now going to accurately estimate sales volume and justify your estimate. You will base your estimate on existing facts, adjusted for your project's unique characteristics and extrapolated into the future.

IDENTIFYING YOUR MARKET

Identifying the market for your project and establishing the credibility of your market definition are critical to selling your project to potential investors. Credibility for your market definition is established by using appropriate methods for researching the market and by explaining and documenting those methods in a manner that will convince potential investors that you have presented a true and complete picture of the potential market for your project.

It is relatively easy to determine the size and characteristics of the market for your project. Start with the old saying, "there is nothing new under the sun." No matter how revolutionary your project's goods or services seem to you, they will almost always be just a different method of performing an existing task or providing an existing service. The easiest way to identify the market your project is in is to analyze your competition. Which businesses will be hurt by your project? When you know your competition you know where to look for statistics on the size and composition of your market.

Once you've identified your market, you can begin to identify and examine its characteristics: Who are the major competitors currently serving your market? Who are the customers? What is the total dollar volume of sales, locally, statewide, and nationally? What is the seasonality of your market? The answers to these and the many other questions concerning your market are most easily obtained by asking people who are now or who have recently been involved in your market. Suppliers will talk about customers. Custom-

ers will talk about suppliers. People in a market know almost
everything (even information which is supposed to be con-
fidential) about competitors, market growth, market potential, etc., and they are not as reluctant to talk to you as you
might think. (Ex-employees can be especially eager to talk
about their former employer's business.) Information on the
market will also be available in reference books at your local
library, or from trade associations connected with your
market. For some large projects, where the required investment amounts are large, potential investors may insist that
formal, scientific market research be obtained through a
professional market research firm.

Obtaining information about a market is called market
research. All market research, whatever the cost and who-
ever is performing it, has the same objective: determining the
number of units of your product or service that can be sold,
and at what price per unit. Those two factors are the basis for
your assumptions regarding projected sales volume.

Market research can be as comprehensive as a formal
questionnaire given to thousands of potential customers at a
cost of several hundred thousand dollars, or it can be as
simple as asking a competitor's sales clerk whether sales
have been good during the last shift. Market research can
easily be very expensive and time-consuming because you
are never certain that you have the correct conclusions.
Absolute accuracy in market research could never be attained unless you questioned every person about your project. Obviously, you cannot afford the cost of such an effort,
but, more importantly, you cannot afford the time it would
take.

Fortunately, the information necessary to draw conclusions about the market for your project can, with 80% to 90%
reliability, be obtained fairly quickly at relatively low cost.
Properly prepared surveys with as few as 200 to 300 respon-
dents provide up to 90% confidence that the results shown

are applicable to the population as a whole. For most projects and investors, this level of market research will suffice.

Whatever the level of market research you employ, you must accurately describe and document your research methods and results in your proposal. The description of your research must contain enough detail to provide a credible base for your assumptions concerning the sales volume projected in your financing proposal.

PROJECTING MARKET SHARE

Researching your market as thoroughly as possible will enable you to estimate the impact your project will have on your market. What will be your project's share, or percent, of your market? If you know the total size of your market, and you know the market share of your project, you can easily compute the total sales for your project. Problems arise when you do not really know the size of your market, which can cause your estimate of market share for your project to be inaccurate. A small error in those numbers can have a huge impact on your sales estimates. You must be extremely careful to gather as much information as you can before you reach any conclusions.

Your project's market share will depend on how and where your project's products or services fit into your market among the competing products and services. In order to adequately project market share, you must be able to answer many questions, including: Where will the market share come from? Which competitor(s) will lose market share to make room for your project? What will be their reaction to the competition from your project? What happens to your project if the competition lowers prices to keep you out of the market? What will cause customers to switch to you from their old suppliers?

The answers to most questions about where you will get

your market share can be found in the statistical analysis of the growth of the total market. In many cases, the dollar volume of sales projected for your project is less than the dollar volume of growth projected for the total market. This means that your project can reach its projected volume, while your competitors still experience sales growth. When this situation exists, the reaction of the competition to your project will generally be minimal. Note that if projected market growth is expected to provide the volume necessary for your entry into the market, you must be able to document the historical trends to support the growth projections.

In those instances where the projected sales volume of your project cannot be covered by market growth because your projected total sales are greater than the expected growth in your market, you must address the question of how you will deal with your competitors' reaction to your entry into their market. What makes your products or services superior or preferable to theirs? Can your project survive a price war? Can you really take your competitors' customers? If you say you can, you must have facts that support your contention.

Customers switch to new suppliers of products or services because of price or quality. However, successful selling of new products or services usually involves lower price, because proving that the quality of your products or services is better than your competitors' is much more difficult than showing a lower price.

PROJECTING THE PRICE
OF YOUR PRODUCT OR SERVICE

The price that you can charge for your products or services has three limiting factors: 1) perceived value by the customer (you can't charge more for something than the customer thinks it is worth); 2) your cost to provide the product or service (you can't sell a product or service for less than it costs to provide it); and 3) competition (you can't charge more for your product or service than competing businesses charge for the same products or services). Your product or service must satisfactorily meet all three limits on price: you must sell at a price that your customers think is fair, that is higher than your cost, and that is equal to or lower than that charged by your competitors.

Of the three components of price, two can be known with some precision. You can know your cost to provide your product or service, and you can know what your competitors are charging for the same product or service. The third component, customers' perceived value, cannot be known with the same level of reliability. However, you can assume that the customers' perceived value of a product or service is equal or very close to the price currently being charged by your competitors. Thus, as a practical matter, you have only two limiting factors involved in the determination of the price you can charge for your product or service: your cost to provide the product or service, and the price your competition is charging for the same product or service.

If the price determined by these two factors is acceptable—that is, if the price charged by your competitors exceeds your cost to provide the product or service by an amount sufficient to generate the profit necessary to successfully operate your project—then no further research need be performed to establish your unit price. Fortunately, for most projects, the two factors of unit cost and competitors' price will usually be in agreement, or close to agreement, making the justification for the assumption of unit price a simple matter of documenting those two factors.

On the other hand, if the cost to provide your product or service exceeds your competitors' price, you have three alternatives: 1) revise your methods of providing the product or service to reduce your costs; 2) convince your customers to pay a higher price for your product or service than they are willing to pay to your competitors; or 3) abandon your project. Remember that should you choose option 2), charging a unit price higher than that of your competition, you will need significant explanation of the reasons you think customers will pay more for your product or service than for those of your competitors. Your potential investors will need convincing that you can alter the pricing structure of your market.

Many times the projected sales for a project are minuscule in relation to the total market. In such cases it is not necessary to take customers from competitors in order to meet sales projections. This is often true when the project involves retail sales. But, even in those cases, there must still be facts to document the projections of sales volume. Such facts include surveys of potential customers, traffic counts near the prospective location for your project, and the sales volume of comparably sized competitors. (Note: If projected sales volume exceeds the sales volume of any of those competitors by a significant amount, you must again be prepared to justify your reasons for projecting such performance.)

Another factor affecting sales volume is the method of selling. Is the product sold at retail or wholesale? Does it require direct salesmen? Is advertising critical to the success of your project? What method of distribution will be utilized? Have you taken the necessary steps to enter that distribution system? If your product is to be sold through grocery or retail stores, have you evaluated and solved the problems of becoming an approved vendor for them? (For example, it is very difficult to sell new products, or products from a new company, to some chains, like Sears or K-Mart.)

PROJECTING SALES VOLUME

By now, you know that in order to determine whether your project has the potential for profitable operation, you must accurately project sales volume. You must gather all the facts available to you and base your projections on those facts. If you find that the sales projections based on the facts will not support your project, you must find another project. If the sales are not there, nothing can save your project.

Sales volume is so critical to the success of your project, and sales estimates are so subject to error, that I recommend, for projection purposes, you reduce your best estimate of sales by at least 10%. If your project is profitable at that level of sales, there is a good chance it will succeed. If, however, your project is not profitable at that reduced level of sales, there is a good chance it will not succeed. To assume that somehow the necessary sales volume will be achieved is to ensure that your project will sink like a stone, taking your own investment and that of your investors with it.

Another reason for conservatively projecting sales volume is that when Murphy's Law takes effect (and it will), you will have an additional cushion against shortfalls in actual sales volume. The more conservative your sales projections, the better your chances to meet them. This is especially true if your sales projections greatly exceed the volumes needed to support the investment you need.

If this is the case for your project, you should not show sales projections in excess of the volume needed. Investors are happy when actual sales beat projections. On the other hand, investors react very poorly when sales do not meet projections. Be as conservative as you can in your estimates of sales volumes.

All this seems straightforward and logical. After all, projections should be based on known facts. Unfortunately, many entrepreneurs present investors with financing proposals containing projections of sales volume that are not based on facts. The owner of a project may simply calculate the expenses involved in the project—manufacturing, selling, and administration—add in a profit factor (perhaps a nice yearly income for the owner), and make the assumption that sales volume will equal the expenses—kind of a reverse breakeven analysis. Such projections have no credibility, but they appear more frequently than they should.

Another improper method of estimating sales volume starts with a well documented projection of the first year's sales. First year projections are then "adjusted" by arbitrary and unsupported percentage increases in sales. Perhaps it is assumed that there will be a 6% annual percentage increase in sales after inflation, and it is also assumed that there will be another 6% increase annually due to inflation. Now you have a 12% annual increase in sales. By the fifth year of projections, the project has excellent sales levels and shows a very healthy-looking set of income statements. But there was never any justification for assuming that 6% increase in sales each year (except that it is small enough to appear conservative). In truth, there is no real evidence that the project will even keep pace with inflation. This method of projecting sales must lead to disappointments because there is no justification or research in the assumptions.

When these or similar improper methods of projecting sales are used, it is usually obvious to an investor. Therefore, if you use them, most investors will not provide funding for your project. Sometimes, however, improper methods of projecting sales are harder to spot. For instance, an owner dissatisfied with the profits shown by the project when using the sales projections that result from proper market analysis and research, may simply "bump" the numbers by a percent or two (or three).

An extra percentage point or two of market share or increase in sales can result in a dramatic increase in sales volume for a project over the five years of projections. And because the increase in percentage is small, it is difficult to spot such "bumps" or adjustments. However, the "bump" has no basis in fact and ultimately the project will not realize the last one or two percentage points of sales that were projected by the "bump." And since the last few percentage points of sales are often the profits for the project, failing to meet the sales projected by the "bump" will almost always mean that the project will fail.

OUTLINING A MARKETING STRATEGY

Your analysis of your market, which is the basis for your projections of unit sales and unit price, is the foundation for your projection of sales volume, the single most important factor in the success or failure of your project. It is not enough to merely document the facts about unit pricing and market share you have gathered during your market research. If you cannot convince enough customers to buy your product or service, your projections will not be met, and your project will not survive. You must show your investors why potential customers will actually buy your product or service. You must outline your marketing strategy.

There are many methods of marketing: media advertising; point-of-sale displays; direct mail; sales calls; power lunches; golf matches; etc. All are valid to some extent with some types of customers. The marketing method you select must be related to your product or service and your method of distributing it.

Your market research identified your potential customers. Your marketing strategy will be based on the demographic characteristics of your potential customers. For example, if you are planning to sell to businesses rather than to the public at large, your marketing strategy will more likely be individual salesmen calling on the purchasing agents of those businesses rather than a series of advertise-ments on television and vice-versa.

When developing your marketing strategy, keep in mind that only when the ultimate consumer, or end user, is convinced to buy your product or service can you consider your product or service sold. If you sell to some middleman, it is easy to make the mistake of thinking that a sale to a middleman (a store, a marketing representative, a broker, etc.) is a sale that will not be returned, and which will be repeated. However, if the end users do not buy from your middleman, your product will not get repeat sales. And if that is the case, your project will die.

Your marketing strategy will almost always resemble that of your competition. If your competitors advertise, your advertising will be comparable to theirs, both in media used and frequency. In such cases, your discussion of your marketing strategy will include your advertising strategy. The support for your advertising strategy will include an analysis of your competitors' media selection and advertis-ing budget.

The advertising budget for your new project can be difficult to establish. Advertising is often budgeted as a percent of sales volume. But your project has no sales volume as yet, and your projected volume for the first few years will most certainly be lower than in later years. Instead of a percent of sales, then, you may budget a specific dollar amount for advertising, based perhaps on the amount spent by your competitors. In some cases, the dollars spent on advertising during the introductory period for a product or service might even exceed sales dollars during that period.

The choice of the advertising medium to use will greatly affect the advertising budget. Each advertising medium has its own cost parameters, usually related to the number of potential customers reached. Broadcast media (television, radio, cable networks, etc.) tend to be more costly than print media (newspapers, magazines, etc.), mainly because the frequency (or number) of ads run on broadcast media tends to be much higher. Single advertisements placed in press publications can be more expensive than a single showing of a commercial on television, but the number of showings of commercials usually makes television advertising more expensive in total.

Each advertising medium used also provides the product with an image. Your choice of media will depend in part on the image you desire for your product or service, which in turn will depend on your potential customers' image of themselves or their companies.

Advertising, as a category, also includes collateral materials. These are the catalogs, brochures, posters, discount coupons, flyers, in-store displays, endorsements, samples, trade fairs, etc., used in conjunction with your other advertising. These items can add up to quite a bit of money if used in any quantities. If your advertising strategy employs collateral materials, you must be sure to budget a dollar amount for the cost of such items.

Describe your advertising strategy accurately and completely so that your investors can see that you have thought through the factors that affect both your project's approach to advertising and the amount you have established as your advertising budget. It is accepted as one of the "truths" in business that advertising and sales are directly related—more advertising dollars result in more sales and fewer advertising dollars result in fewer sales.

But no one—not even the largest advertising agency—can claim to be able to predict how many dollars of sales will be generated by each dollar of advertising. If your advertising strategy is not fully documented and supported, your investors will more than likely "suggest" a lower amount for your advertising budget in order to reduce costs. They would see this as a reduction in the amount of investment required from them. Such reductions in advertising expense can be fatal when you begin to operate your project.

One of the projects I worked on involved the preparation of financial projections for a new product, and the marketing strategy and budget for the introduction of the product. This case was unusual, in that the owner had quite a bit of control over the investor (as long as the projections looked "all right"), but it is still a useful illustration of what happens when projections and budgets are adjusted to agree with predetermined goals.

This particular product was a food product, and the distribution and sales methods were quite clear—sales at retail through grocery stores. We developed sales projections based on our marketing strategy, which was derived from discussions with members of the industry who had prior experience with new food product introductions. Our financial projections called for a substantial advertising budget and showed a net loss for the first year.

However, the owner of the project was determined that **his** product would not ever show a loss, even in its first year, although first-year losses on new products are common in the food industry. In fact, many new food products lose money for two or three years, because the advertising expenses necessary to sell the new product to consumers tend to be so high, and the margins in grocery products tend to be so thin, that the profits from sales do not cover expenses until the product is fairly well established.

In any event, this owner did not want to show his investor a projected loss, and insisted that we reduce advertising expense and increase projected sales in his financing proposal, until the project showed a profit. These changes were made in spite of our strenuous objections and predictions of disaster, but he was the owner, and he won out. After all, it was his project. (Please note that without such control over the investor, this owner probably could not have overridden the advice of his consultants in such a manner.)

As you might expect, the adjusted sales estimates were not attained, mainly because the reduced advertising budget kept the product a secret from consumers. The introduction of the product was severely impaired, and, in fact, the product never did recover. The product did not make the money projected in the financing proposal, so there was an "unexpected" loss. The owner won the battle of the earnings projections, but he lost the war of the new product, lost his investor's money, and ultimately lost the support of his investor. How much better off would everyone have been if realistic sales projections had been used?

If the owner had only had the sense to stick to the original advertising budget, and gone ahead and absorbed the projected first and second year losses, I believe the product would now be firmly established in its home market and on its way to national distribution. We were able to make some inroads in the market in spite of the lack of advertising. But not enough money was invested to cover the first- and second-year operating losses. The unwillingness to face the reality of early losses killed the product.

In discussing your advertising strategy, you must recognize that literally every potential investor is exposed to advertising, and each and every one "knows" what constitutes effective advertising. Investors may know intellectually that their opinion of effective advertising is subjective and does not necessarily apply to a particular project, but they "know what they like," and they are putting up the money.

To reduce the risk that you will be forced to use someone else's favorite advertising techniques, your advertising strategy must be based on proven strategies successfully used in similar situations and must be fully documented. If you choose to use an advertising strategy different from that used by your competitors, you must be well prepared to defend it against the "suggestions" of your investors.

PROJECTING MARKETING COSTS

Marketing is more than just advertising. Of course, for those projects where the product or service is sold directly to consumers, advertising is usually the largest marketing expense by far. But for those projects where the product or service is sold to businesses, direct advertising expense may be minimal.

The largest marketing expense in that case might be the salaries of the direct sales force, or the sales commissions for a group of manufacturer's representatives. Therefore, whatever marketing strategy you choose, you must document the reasons behind that choice, explaining it in sufficient detail to convince an investor that you know enough to make the correct choice and that, in fact, the correct choice was made.

Marketing expenses are usually budgeted as a percentage of sales. Advertising, sales commissions, or sales payroll are all subject to industry norms as a percent of sales. If your project uses advertising, it will probably exceed those norms in its first year or two, because sales have not reached their potential. However, during the initial years, the amounts you plan to spend on advertising should not exceed the dollar amount that would be spent by a company the size you expect yours to be.

Advertising expense is most easily documented by asking one or more advertising agencies for their proposals for your advertising campaigns. They will be happy to provide you with a proposal and will do most of the necessary research on advertising in your industry for you.

Sales commissions are usually based on a percent of sales. Your industry will have a "normal" sales commission percent, so that projecting this expense is simple. If you plan on using salaried salespeople, the percent of sales represented by sales salaries will usually not exceed the normal sales commission percent. If it does, you will need facts from within your industry to justify the level of sales salaries.

PROJECTING OPERATING COSTS

You aren't finished gathering information. Now that you know what your sales volume and marketing costs will be, you need to document your costs of operation. The costs of operation include the cost of goods sold—the costs to manufacture or otherwise prepare your product or service for sale. You must also document administrative costs—office rent, accounting, legal, office salaries, insurance, supplies, and the like. If there are any significant costs that don't fit into the above categories, you will show them separately.

The costs of your project are much easier to document than are sales projections. Each category of expense can be costed with precision, based on the number of units to be used or some other measurable factor. Cost of goods sold is determined by the units sold multiplied by the cost per unit. The cost per unit will depend on the type of product or service provided by your project.

If you manufacture your products, cost of goods sold has two components: variable and fixed. The variable cost per unit is determined by adding the cost of the materials used in each unit to the cost of the labor to make each unit. The fixed cost per unit is the pro rata cost of the machinery and equipment, etc., used in the manufacturing of your product. Depreciation, plant rent, utilities, and supervision are included therein.

If you purchase products for resale, at either the wholesale or retail levels, cost of goods sold is calculated as a percentage of sales. This percentage is determined by the industry. Cost of goods sold in a retail shop are typically 45% to 50% of sales. In a wholesale operation, the cost of goods sold will be closer to 75% to 80% of sales. But selling and administrative costs are generally a much lower percent of sales in a wholesale operation compared to a retail shop, thus net profit as a percent of sales can be very close for both a wholesale and retail operation, even though the cost of goods percentage varies greatly.

If your project provides a service, cost of goods sold may not be a meaningful number. The materials used and the labor to apply the materials in a service operation are usually a small percentage of sales. However, selling and administrative expenses tend to be a greater percent of sales, so that the net profit as a percent of sales is comparable to other types of operations.

Whatever product or service your project provides, the variable components of sales—those that increase in direct proportion to sales—will generally have the same relationship to sales as those of your competitors. For example, in a sit-down restaurant the cost of food is usually about 37% of sales, but in a fast-food restaurant the cost of food is closer to 25% of sales. The cost of labor to serve and prepare the food runs about 12% to 15% in a sit-down restaurant versus 23% to 25% in a fast-food restaurant (because of tips in the sit-down restaurant). Every industry has its own percent-to-sales parameters for the major items of variable expense. Talking with people in your industry will allow you to quickly establish the percentage parameters for variable expenses in your project.

Most other cost elements are equally easy to determine. Whether it is the average hourly wage rate in your industry, utility costs, rent, insurance, or any of the other costs of doing business, the information is readily available. A few conversations with someone who has worked in the industry will yield the information, either as absolute numbers, or as a percent of sales.

It is more important that you identify all cost elements than that you be absolutely correct in your estimate of each cost. An incorrect cost element can be noticed and corrected in a review of your proposal, but a missing cost element can be very hard to spot. Depending on the industry, certain cost elements that you would not normally think of as major might be significant. For instance, if your project involves manufacturing, your workers' comprehensive insurance coverage (mandatory by law) can be as much as 20% of your payroll costs, while in a retail environment, workers' comprehensive insurance will be closer to 6% or 7% of payroll. And if you manufacture products, it is likely that payroll will be a greater percentage of sales than in a retail situation, compounding the effect if you forgot to include an amount for workers' comprehensive insurance.

Murphy's law is at work here, too. If you do happen to miss a cost element, it will probably be major, and when that cost is found and added in to your projections, your profit margins may be reduced to barely acceptable levels.

You must identify, quantify, and justify every revenue and expense element of your project. You will include a narrative description of every element representing 5% or more of the total revenues or expenses. You will have to prove that you did your homework and that you understand all facets of your project.

It is especially important that you do not ignore anything. Investors have one characteristic that can prove fatal to your project: if they see one single item which they do not like or do not believe, they will not believe anything else in your proposal. The more you know, and the more you can prove that you know, the more likely you will be to convince an investor that you can safely handle his or her money in your project.

THE FORMAL
REQUEST FOR MONEY

As we noted in the beginning of this book, every business or project has made at least one request for money. Someone put up the cash to pay for the assets and operations of the business until it could generate sufficient cash flow on its own. And money does not just appear; you must at least ask for it. Asking for money in this context calls for preparing a financing proposal. This chapter tells you how to prepare a good financing proposal. It is a stand-alone part of the book and can be used by itself to help you in your search for financing.

THE IMPORTANCE OF FINANCING PROPOSALS

Formal requests for money, or financing proposals, are prepared whenever any project cannot fulfill its own cash needs and requires outside cash. New projects almost always need outside cash to finance the start-up, but even existing businesses sometimes need outside cash to finance a new project or to expand their operations. Existing businesses occasionally raise cash by financing receivables or inventory, but such types of financing are usually handled with a secured loan from a bank or other financial institution and are not the subject of our discussion. We are concerned here with financing your new project through long-term loans or equity investments from outside investors.

Before they will provide financing, outside investors

want an explanation of your project and a projection of the profits and cash flow which will result from its successful operation. They also want evidence that you have researched your project thoroughly and have anticipated potential problems.

You will meet those requirements through your financing proposal. The explanation of your project and the projection of its profits are the two main purposes of your financing proposal. Your proposal must be complete and well written in order to create a climate of credibility. The credibility of your financing proposal is the key to your success in obtaining funding for your project.

Anyone who has had the opportunity to examine several financing proposals, or "business plans," will agree that proposals can and do range in quality from well-written and comprehensive to woefully incomplete. Interestingly, the quality of a financing proposal does not necessarily increase or decrease with the size and complexity of the project, or with the amount of money sought. Financing proposals for projects requiring relatively small amounts of money are often much more comprehensive than are financing proposals for projects which require millions of dollars. Some financing proposals are so poorly written it seems almost as if the owner is daring the investor to turn down the request for money to justify complaints about the unreasonableness of investors.

At seminars attended by representatives of venture capital firms, the participants are of nearly unanimous opinion that one of the biggest needs of the venture capital industry is better quality financing proposals. According to these representatives, the majority of the financing proposals submitted to their firms tend to be incomplete, unorganized, and poorly written. While a poorly prepared financing proposal is not necessarily fatal to a project, it does place a project at a competitive disadvantage against projects with more complete and better written financing proposals. It is hard enough to find financing under the best conditions. Why run the risk of having your proposal rejected simply because of style and content?

The major problem with many financing proposals is that most owners have never written one before and may never do so again. They are not aware that investors need so many facts and so much explanation. Typically, owners become so immersed in their project that it is hard for them to realize that other people do not understand it as well as they do. They write a proposal full of jargon, making leaps from one aspect of their project to another without laying a proper foundation so that readers may understand it.

In most cases, the owners can answer any and all questions about their project—its market, its competition, its manufacturing costs, etc.—but simply lack the skills necessary to develop the information into a coherent financing proposal. Owners who have developed projects tend to be intelligent and willing to learn, but their interests lie in running their project, not in writing a financing proposal. Incomplete and poorly written financing proposals are often the result of an owner simply not realizing how important a well-written financing proposal is to the success of the project.

The sole function of a financing proposal is to provide the answers to the potential investor's two basic questions:

1) "How much money is needed?" and

2) "What do I get in return?"

All information contained in your proposal is intended to address aspects of one or the other of the two basic questions. Questions such as : "What is the project about?" "When is the money needed?" "Where does the money go?" and "What are the inventory requirements?" are all related

to the first basic question—"How much money is needed?"—
while questions such as: "Does the owner know how to run
his project?" "What is the risk?" "What are the repayment
terms?" "What is the rate of interest?" and "How much
equity do I get?" are related to the second basic question—
"What do I get in return?"

We will discuss how to answer these two basic questions and all their various aspects through a well-structured,
comprehensive financing proposal. The required elements
of the financing proposal will be covered in enough detail
that you will be able to prepare your own proposal, or be able
to tell whether your consultants have prepared a financing
proposal that is good enough to help you convince investors
to put up money for your project.

A good financing proposal will not guarantee that you
will get the money you seek, but it gives you a leg up with
investors. A poor financing proposal, on the other hand, puts
you at such a disadvantage with investors that your project
may not be able to overcome it. And poor financing proposals are so needless. It is not difficult to prepare a good
proposal. It is a step-by-step process. If you follow the steps
in this chapter, you will have a good financing proposal.

THE ELEMENTS OF A FINANCING PROPOSAL

The major elements that must be included and covered
in a financing proposal are as follow:

Overview, or Executive Summary

Project Description

Market Description

Marketing Plan

Capital Requirements and Construction Schedule

Personnel

Management

Financial Projections

Conflicts of Interests, Fees, and Risks

Return on Investment

The order of the sections above is one I prefer, but the structure of your own project may suggest a different order. You are packaging your project to sell to an investor, so you will put your best foot forward. You may alter the order shown above, but every element must be covered somewhere in your proposal.

Before we get deeper into this discussion, we should explain our use of the term "financing proposal" throughout, instead of one of the other terms that you will hear as you prepare your proposal. "Financial plan," "business plan," and "financing proposal" are three terms that are sometimes used interchangeably. Technically, "financial plan" refers only to the portion of the financing proposal containing the projected financial statements and their underlying assumptions. "Business plan" is more comprehensive, including the financial portions and certain narrative portions often found in "financing proposals." But a "business plan" is many times presented as an internal document, and as such would not contain many of the elements that are necessary to a complete "financing proposal" presented to outside investors for the purpose of raising money.

As you get deeper into the process, you will hear other terms, oftentimes buzzword-type combinations of the words in the above terms, such as "financial business plan" or "business financing plan." You will soon learn to define such terms for yourself by the context of their use.

We will discuss the sections of your financing proposal in the order in which they I listed them above. However, their order of appearance in the proposal is not the order in which you will do the work necessary to prepare them. You will prepare the financial projections and the marketing plan first. They are the heart of your proposal. You, yourself, have to know whether you can market your product or service and whether your project will make money before you begin to prepare a formal proposal to present your project to investors.

THE OVERVIEW

Your financing proposal will be arranged in the order that best leads the potential investor to an understanding of your project and its profit potential. You do not need to present your financial projections first. Investors assume your financial projections show a good profit, or you would not be coming to them for money.

You should start off by demonstrating that you have done enough research to create the necessary credibility to cause an investor to believe that your project has the "right stuff" to meet its projected profit levels. Also, an investor doesn't want to waste any more time than is necessary in order to determine whether or not there is any interest in your project. The first section in your financing proposal will, therefore, be the "Overview" or "Executive Summary."

The Overview is a well written summary of the rest of your proposal. It will be three to five pages long. (Any longer and it ceases to be a summary.) Start with a description of the product or service provided by your project. What is it? What does it do? What need is filled? Is it a copy of an existing product or service? Is there patent protection? What makes your product or service salable? What is unusual or unique about your product or service? Is it a lower cost or better performer than existing similar products or services? You have to sell your project to investors by making them see the sales potential for your product or service.

Your investor, as we discussed, wants to know the answers to the two basic questions. The answers must be in your Overview. Tell the investor how much money you need and what you will spend it on. Also, summarize the basic financial information-sales, profits, and return on investment—in a form that is readily understood by the investor, usually in a narrative form.

If your Overview is not understandable or complete, it may well be the only part of your proposal that the investor reads. You should think of the Overview as the hook that makes an investor want to read more about your project.

When investors do read on through your proposal, they must be able to find every fact and number you included in the Overview. Everything mentioned in the Overview section, from a marketing technique to a profit number, must be discussed at length in the body of your proposal. Nothing kills an interview or a presentation as quickly as having a potential investor look at you and say, "I noticed in your Overview that you project a 35% return on investment, but I can't find that number in the financial section." Or, "You say you're going to sell your iceboxes to the Eskimos, but you don't say how you're going to advertise them."

The Overview is your opening shot. If the investor reads anything, it will be your Overview. Make it brief, complete, and coherent to maximize the chance that the investor will want to further examine your proposal and allow you to make a personal presentation.

THE PROJECT DESCRIPTION

The first section in the main portion of your financing proposal is the Project Description. The organization of your project description section will vary depending on the nature of your project. Emphasize those areas that have the greatest impact on the success of your project.

For instance, the location of facilities is of primary importance to a project involving retail sales, while employee training and selection can be of lesser stature. For a project involving manufacturing, on the other hand, location is not so important, but qualified, trained employees can have great impact. The characteristics of your project will determine how you describe the project to potential investors.

Outline the history of your project up to now. How did you get the idea? (Briefly, please. None of those, "I had a dream..." stories.) What have you already accomplished to help assure the success of your project? This may take several pages, if the history of your project is interesting. If your project is new and has no history, you must still cover the origination of the concept, and describe the various elements of the project in some detail.

Include a discussion of the characteristics of your product or service. Is there manufacturing or assembly required? If so, cover the type, location, and size of manufacturing and warehousing facilities required. What facilities are required for delivery of the product or service? Is your project affected by seasonal variations? As your project matures through the first five years shown in the financial projections, how do the above elements change? How will you handle the changes?

THE MARKET DESCRIPTION

After you have described your project, you will define the market for it. You need to identify the market for your project in enough detail that an investor can understand how your project fits into its market. The section of your proposal containing your market description will help demonstrate the depth of your research efforts.

Clearly identify the type of customer your project will serve, how many customers there are, which competitors currently serve your customers, what is the market share of each of those competitors, and why your project's product or service will attract customers. Will it take existing customers from competitors, or will it generate its own new customers? What percentage of the existing market do you project for your project? (Note: If the market share you calculate is more than 10% or if your market share is larger than that of your largest competitor, investors will need extra convincing if they are to believe your projections.)

Your purpose here is to prove to the investor that the market for your project exists; that it can be separated from other markets by the characteristics of its customers, products, or services; and that it is large enough to support your project's entry into the market without requiring the removal of one or more competitors. Investors will not readily believe that your project will be able to run existing companies out of business.

Your project may represent the first product or service in a new market, or one of the early entries in a young market. In such cases, you will have to devote a substantial amount of this section to just proving the existence of your market. Your market research will need to be more definitive and should probably be performed by a recognized research organization. And your product or service will need to be fairly attractive.

In this context, the term "attractive" can have two meanings. There is the objective judgment that the product has a niche in a market, based on research and competitive conditions. And there is the subjective judgment, on the part of potential investors, concerning whether or not they themselves would use the product. It is amazing how much more "attractive" projects get for investors when the products or services they offer are useful to the investors themselves.

Investors can see the potential for your product or service much more easily if they are potential customers.

As a practical matter, your project will probably fit into an existing market that has enough total sales volume to absorb the revenues of your project without undue strain on the market or on any individual competitor. Almost every new product or service, even a high-tech invention, replaces or improves upon one or more existing products or services. You must be clear about the products or services with which your project competes so that your market definition is accurate and easily understood by the investor.

The Marketing Plan

You have defined your market and shown that there is adequate room in that market for your project. Now you must show your investor that you know how to penetrate your market. A comprehensive discussion of your marketing plan will accomplish that. Establishing credibility for your marketing plan is important, if not critical, to the success of your quest for funding. Your description of your market and your marketing plan are necessary to support your sales and revenue projections in the financial section of your proposal.

Your marketing plan must prove to an investor that you have examined all potential problems and have the required solutions. You must convince your investor that you **can** meet your sales projections, and your project **will** make money. And it will do so because you know how to sell your product or service.

The first step in describing your marketing plan is to outline your research on the marketing strategies employed by your competitors. What is their marketing budget? Is it based on a percent of sales, or is the amount fixed? What percentage of their total marketing budget is used for adver-

tising? For sales payrolls and/or commissions? For bro-
chure printing and distribution? For catalog printing? For
travel? For trade shows? For samples?

If they advertise, what amount or percentage is spent on
media (television, radio, magazines, billboards, newspapers,
etc.)? Which media do they use? Which television shows?
Which radio stations? Which magazines? Which trade
publications? Which section of the newspaper? Is their sales
staff made up of employees or outside, commissioned sales
reps? What trade shows do they attend? Where do they
travel? Do they take customers on trips? You must answer
all the questions, regardless of the size of your project or the
amount of money you seek.

You will find when you look at competitors' marketing
budgets that they are all very similar. In the same industry,
most businesses spend the same percentage of sales or the
same fixed amount on marketing. Your marketing budget
will be similar, also, or you must explain how you have
discovered something that everyone else in the industry has
missed. The percent of their marketing budget that each
allocates to the different elements of marketing will also be
pretty much the same throughout the industry, although you
can expect more variation in the individual elements of a
marketing budget than there will be in the total amount
budgeted for marketing. Your marketing budget must be
within the norms for the industry, or you must document the
reasons for the variations.

As you outline your marketing strategy, do not forget
distribution. You must get your product or service to the
place where your customers can buy it. All the advertising
in the world will not generate one sale if your product or
service is not readily available to your consumer.

To paraphrase Thomas Edison, selling is 5% good ideas
and 95% distribution. If your product or service is unavail-
able to your customers, they will use an alternative. If your

system of distribution requires your customer to call you, even on an "800" number, you will not maximize your sales. Here again, a good solution is to do what your competitors do, or improve on their methods. But you must address how you intend for your project to get orders for your products or services.

Your marketing strategy should be fairly detailed. How much money will you spend for each type of marketing? Which specific media will you use? Which sales rep organizations? Which advertising agency, and what are their qualifications? If you have samples of the types of advertisements you will run, insert copies in this section.

By doing all this, you are proving you have covered all aspects of marketing your project. An investor should realize after reading your plan, that you have researched the marketing of your project in enough depth to be sure that your project will meet its sales projections. That is the purpose of this section of your proposal.

CAPITAL REQUIREMENTS
AND CONSTRUCTION SCHEDULING

If your project includes substantial capital additions, you will need a separate section on capital requirements and construction scheduling. (If your project does not utilize a large amount of fixed assets, the capital requirements section can be discussed in the project description and included in the assumptions in the financial section.)

Remember, you are still establishing your credibility with potential investors, so it is not enough to simply note that you need a building somewhere with a bunch of equipment in it. You need to provide a detailed list of the specific equipment required by your project, and the specific amount of real estate—buildings and land—needed to contain the equipment.

Again, the best source for your list of capital requirements is your competition. What real estate do they use? What equipment do they use? Do they rent/lease or own? Are there efficiencies you intend to introduce into the process that will change your capital requirements from those of your competitors? If so, what are they?

If you have specialized needs—a new building, for instance—you should identify the architectural firm you will use and include preliminary renderings of your proposed facilities. Your architects can also provide you with rough cost estimates for the facilities and a preliminary schedule of construction.

You might already own the land or have an option on it. The building may already exist. If so, you will need to show the value you place on those assets. If you are going to lease space, list the location, the number of square feet you need, and the cost per square foot.

Any equipment you need should be listed, the manufacturer identified, and the cost and delivery schedule shown. If you already own the equipment or are going to buy used equipment, show the cost in this section. If equipment will be leased, show the terms and the delivery schedule.

A schedule for the construction of buildings and delivery of equipment is important, not only because it shows when your project will be ready to begin operations, but also because it shows the investor when you will need money for progress payments as your project is built.

All the above items are part of your research. An investor will expect you to know how much you are going to spend on the facilities required to operate your project. Include copies of any preliminary plans or drawings you might have. Anything in your proposal that indicates the amount of time and effort you have spent researching all areas of your project helps convince the investor that you are qualified to run your project.

PERSONNEL AND MANAGEMENT

As you perform your research regarding potential sales volume and capital requirements for your project, you will have to know the number of employees you will need to operate your project. A discussion of personnel requirements is an important part of your proposal. The discussion will include a list of employees by position. You will address these questions among others: How many employees do you need? Are they full-time or part-time? Should they be experienced or can they be untrained? Where will you find people with the necessary skills? Will you need to train your employees? Will you have off-season layoffs? How will you handle them? Will you or your relatives be included as employees? How much does each position pay?

One way to present this information is to include an organization chart for your project, showing the different areas of responsibility—manufacturing, sales, administration, etc.—and listing the number of employees in each area, along with the amount of annual payroll for each area.

Part of the personnel for your project will be the management. You will prepare a separate section for this discussion. Who is going to run your project? Probably you will, together with a hand-picked team of qualified executives. How are they qualified? Have they worked in the same industry as your project? How many years have they worked in similar positions? Just as in any other section, your discussion of your executives will be tailored to your project.

All projects need a chief executive officer, a marketing executive, an administrative executive, a financial executive, and an operations executive. If the project is small enough, one person may have more than one function, but if your project is large or if there is a large investment required, investors will expect to see several executives with complementary skills serving in the different executive roles. If your project requires a large number of experienced personnel to make it work, you may need a personnel executive, and, if there is a long period of construction, you may have a construction executive. Any factor which is clearly critical to the success of your project must have an identified individual in charge.

In your project, especially if it is a new project, management might consist solely of you and the other owners. Your team might be missing one or more critical areas of expertise. You might need a good sales executive or a top production person. You are aware of it, but you can't do anything about it until you are funded. You can't hire people unless you can pay them. In such cases, you will note that you are short one or two people and discuss your intentions to hire quality executives upon funding. Know your weaknesses and address them in your discussion on personnel.

In some instances, you might choose to handle some of the requirements for experienced executive talent by using outside consultants in executive capacities and/or on your Board of Directors. There is nothing wrong with this, as long as you can show that the consultants will be available as often as needed by your project, that the fees paid are commensurate with the duties, and that you have a long-range plan to cover the project's executive needs after the consultants have left your project. In any case, if you choose to use outside consultants, you must give a synopsis of their experience, showing why the use of a particular consultant benefits the project.

In the discussion of management, you are showing the investors why your management team should be entrusted with their money. Be as specific and detailed as you can. Reference especially the experience of each member of your team that applies directly to your project. Convince the investor that you and your team are "the guys in the white hats." Remember that before an investor gives you money, there will almost always be a personal interview with your executive team. Your section on management should be prepared with a personal meeting in mind.

FINANCIAL PROJECTIONS

We are now going to discuss the financial projections for your project. This section of the book will tend to be more technical than the rest, because accounting tends to be more structured than most of the other subjects in this book. Not to fear, however. We'll try to keep it simple. And if it still scares the stuffing out of you, you can always hire an accountant/financial expert to prepare your projections. Even if you do use outside help, you should still read these pages so that you will have enough background to be able to tell whether your expert is doing an adequate job.

This discussion contains the list of the financial schedules that must be covered in your financial projections, and the aspects of each schedule that need to be addressed in your proposal. Each financial projection presented must be supported by narrative assumptions. These assumptions explain to investors how you developed your projections and allow them to make their own analysis of the credibility of your projections. We will cover the projected operating results, the projected cash flow, and the projected balance sheet here.

Before covering the individual schedules of your projected financial statements, we need to discuss the period for which you will make projections. The usual period is five years. Investors feel that running projections out five years allows enough time for your project to reach maturity or close to it. But they also realize that projections are merely that—projections—and that the farther you go into the future, the less you can rely on current assumptions. Investors will not usually give any credence to projections beyond five years.

The first two years will be projected by month, or at least by quarter. This shows any seasonality you may predict for sales, and also shows for how many months you expect to have operating losses, and to what extent. Many times a project can show a positive cash flow for an entire year, while the monthly cash flow statements might show that at some time during that year, the project had quite a large negative cash flow requiring additional funds, if only for a short time.

Projections for the last three years of the five will be annual projections, since individual monthly projections tend to lose their credibility beyond 24 months. In addition, your project should be profitable by the end of the first two years, and there should not be any additional capital required during years three through five unless you plan an expansion.

Results of Operations

The first financial schedules will be your projected results of operations (sometimes called projected profit and loss, or projected income statements). The first element in any set of projected operating results is **revenues** or **sales**. How much money will your project generate by providing its products or services to your customers? You will outline here how many units of each product or service will be sold in each of the years for which projections are made, and at what average price for each unit.

Using the same assumptions on unit sales and unit prices you used in your discussion of your market and your marketing plan, you will mathematically calculate your projected revenues. The sum of the sales of each type of product or service will be your projected total revenues.

During each of the first five years of a project, sales usually increase. Part of that increase in sales will be attributable to increased unit sales as the project matures and becomes more successful, and part of the increase in sales will result from price increases due to inflation. You must clearly differentiate between the types of sales increases by listing unit sales by period and noting the annual rate of inflation you predict.

If your project deals with products, either manufactured or purchased for resale at retail or wholesale, the next caption will be **cost of goods sold** or **cost of sales**. Cost of goods sold represents the amount of money you will spend to purchase or manufacture the units you will sell during the period covered by the projection. Your discussion of cost of goods sold will list the number of units sold by type and the cost to produce or buy each unit.

If you manufacture your products, you will show the calculation of the cost to produce each unit, adding the cost of materials used, freight costs, labor and fringe benefits, tooling costs, rent on manufacturing space, utilities used in manufacturing, depreciation on manufacturing equipment, and every other cost directly involved in the manufacture of your products, prorated to each unit. If you purchase your products for resale, you will show the cost of the units, including freight charges.

Cost of goods sold varies directly with sales. One unit of sales requires one unit of cost of goods sold; one hundred units of sales requires one hundred units of cost of goods sold. The projections of cost of goods sold by period will therefore increase directly with sales over the five years covered by your projections, and will include the same two components of increase: increased unit sales, and increased costs due to inflation. Again, you will differentiate between the two types of increases.

If your project provides a service, rather than a product, there will not usually be a cost of goods sold element. The cost of materials, labor, etc. used to provide the services will be shown in the expense portion of the statements, with each in its own expense element.

The next element in your projected results of operations

is **gross margin**. Gross margin is calculated by subtracting cost of goods sold from sales. The gross margin percent to sales should be the same for every period, reflecting the direct variance of cost of goods sold with sales. Your project's gross margin percent to sales will be comparable to that of other businesses that compete with your project. If it is not identical or close to that of your competitors, you must explain why, in great detail, since the gross margin represents the net dollars your project has available to cover **selling, occupancy,** and **administrative** expenses. The greater the gross margin percent, the greater the number of dollars generated by the same level of sales. You will find great interest in your gross margin percent.

Selling expenses are the total of those expenses involved in selling your products or services and delivering those products or services to your customers. Specific expense elements found in this group include **advertising** and **promotion** expense (sometimes shown as a separate group), **selling salaries** and/or **commissions, travel and entertainment** (for sales personnel), **operating supplies** (for projects which provide services), and **delivery costs**.

The magnitude of the specific expense elements will vary depending on the type of product or service offered by your project. For example, advertising and promotion are usually higher when the product or service is sold to the public than when it is sold to other businesses. However, selling salaries and/or commissions, and related travel and entertainment expenses are usually higher when the product or service is sold to a limited number of customers through individual sales calls by salesmen than when the product or service is sold to the general public. When these expense elements are examined individually, and related to the product or service, the relative magnitude of each is usually fairly evident and logical.

Occupancy expenses are dependent on the product or

services offered by your project and the facilities required to present them to your customers. The size, location, and cost of your office, warehouse, or plant, and the necessary utilities expense (electricity, water, gas, etc.) are determined by the needs of each product or service. The specific expense captions usually associated with occupancy include **rent, utilities, property taxes,** etc. These costs are usually considered "fixed," because the amount of expense does not vary with sales, at least in the short term.

General and Administrative expenses include **office salaries** and **fringes, accounting and legal** expense, **insurance, office supplies, office equipment rental, telephone, travel and entertainment** (other than sales), **miscellaneous** expense, and any other expense element which is not attributable to selling expense, occupancy expense or cost of goods sold.

General and administrative expenses (commonly referred to as "G & A" expenses) usually have their own pattern of variation from month to month and year to year, independent of just about everything. Many times your estimate of these expenses for projection purposes will be nothing more than a guess based on your "feel" for the amount. These expenses are frequently minor, in which case the above technique for estimating is allowable. However, in those cases where the expense is large, such as insurance expense, you will need to research the amount and follow the same estimating procedures as for other major expense elements.

Depreciation is based on the amount of capital purchases made in connection with your project, and the useful life of those purchases. Each purchase has its own useful life: a building might be used for 20 years, while an automobile might have a life of three years; office equipment usually lasts five years, but a piece of manufacturing equipment normally has a life of 10 or 15 years.

Depreciation is calculated by listing every capital purchase for your project, determining the useful life and salvage value (if any) of each purchase, and calculating the amount of depreciation for each asset year by year. Adding the individual depreciation amounts by year will provide the total depreciation expense for that year. Dividing the total for a year by 12 will provide the monthly depreciation expense. You should include a detailed list of capital purchases and their useful lives in your explanation of assumptions concerning depreciation. In manufacturing operations, a portion of depreciation expense may be allocated to cost of goods sold. For other types of projects, depreciation expense is a separate line item, usually shown following general and administrative expenses.

Costs and expenses other than cost of goods sold do not always vary with sales. Some, like sales commissions (if applicable), will vary with sales, while others, such as rent, remain constant from month to month. Still others, such as advertising, may "lead" sales. That is, depending on how long it takes to build excitement for your product or service, you could show an increase in advertising a month or two prior to the corresponding increase in sales. There are also expense elements, such as utilities, that have a pattern all their own, without regard to sales. Some expenses can vary because of a decision you make. For example, the rent expense for a fancy office downtown will be higher than that for a small office in a suburban warehouse facility.

The fact that an expense does not vary with sales does not mean you cannot predict it. Just as with other areas of your project, you will find that similar expense categories behave similarly in similar projects. If you know the level of a certain expense in your competitor's business, you can expect that expense to have a proportional level in your project.

In most cases, it is useful to compare expense elements as a percent of sales. For example, if your projected Sales are $10,000, and your projected payroll expense, rent expense and maintenance expense are $1,500, $1,000 and $750, then the percent to sales for each expense is: payroll—15%; rent—10%; and maintenance—7.5%. These percentages can be compared to the percentages experienced by other, similar businesses. If a similar business has sales of $30,000, payroll of $4,200, rent of $3,300 and maintenance of $2,400, then the applicable percents to sales are: payroll—14%; rent—11%; and maintenance—8%. The percentages to sales are comparable, even though the dollar amounts are much different.

Comparing percentages is preferable to comparing dollar amounts because percentages automatically compensate for different sales levels. Making these comparisons of the projected expense levels for your project to those experienced by existing, similar businesses provides you with assurance that your projected expense levels are appropriate.

If you should note a big difference between your project and a similar business in the percent to sales of any expense element, you must examine the reasons for the variation. Is it because your sales are lower, and thus, the percent to sales will be larger until your project's sales grow? Or is it because you are allocating too many or too few dollars to that expense? Be prepared to explain any noticeable variance in expense percentages to sales between your project and existing businesses.

Sometimes you may find during your comparisons that your financial projections do not even include a certain expense element which is found in similar businesses. In such cases, the chances are you have not considered the impact of that expense element on your project. If a significant expense category is overlooked or underestimated, the projected earnings for your project can be dramatically affected. You should review the list of expense elements for your project with actual historical expenses experienced by existing, similar businesses on an element-by-element basis.

Using projected sales, cost of goods sold, and expenses for the five-year period, you can calculate the projected results of operations. **Net earnings from operations** is calculated by subtracting total expenses from gross margin (if applicable), or from sales (if your financial projections do not show gross margin).

In order to calculate projected **net income**, the only item left to project is **income taxes**. However, most projects use a structure that allows income and expense items to "pass through" to the owners and investors for use on their individual income tax returns, so you do not usually have to consider income taxes for the project itself in your projections. If income taxes do play a part in the scenario, they are easy to calculate later.

Cash Flow

In your financial projections section, you will need to include more than the projected results of operations. You will also need to prepare and discuss the projected cash flow from your project. It can be argued that cash flow projections are the heart of your financing proposal, since they show the amount of financing required, the timing of the financing, and the timing of the projected return to investors. This section is where you establish your need for funds from investors and demonstrate your ability to repay them.

As with the projected results of operations, accurate cash flow projections depend on credible assumptions based on facts. Proper documentation of your assumptions is critical to their credibility. The assumptions which are needed for a cash flow projection include estimates of the amount and timing of specific cash uses, the largest of which are usually the capital additions on which your project is based. The section on capital requirements in your financing proposal also contains the construction schedule, which is used to predict the timing of the expenditures for capital additions.

The timing of cash uses other than capital additions will also be documented. Such uses include repayment of loans (new and existing), acquisition of beginning inventories, establishment of beginning cash balances, and prepayment of certain expense items such as insurance and rent.

Earnings projections are prepared on the accrual basis, where sales and expenses are recognized when the transactions occur: when the sale is made or the purchases arrive. The cash flow projections, however, are prepared on the cash basis, where sales and expenses are not recorded until the period in which the cash changes hands. On the cash basis, a sale is not a sale until you receive the money, and a purchase does not occur until you pay for it. Thus the same event is usually recorded in one period on the accrual basis and in another period on the cash basis.

These discrepancies are called **timing differences**. Timing differences arise when there is a difference between the period in which a transaction occurs requiring a transfer of cash from you or to you and the period in which the actual transfer of cash from you or to you occurs. When bringing earnings information forward from the projected results of operations to the cash flow projections, the timing differences between the accrual basis and the cash basis must be taken into account.

The process of adjusting transactions recorded on the accrual basis to the cash basis is not difficult, but involves separate calculations for each type of transaction. For example, payment for sales, in those companies which extend credit, is almost never received until the month following the sale, and, depending on billing practices, might not be received for two or even three months following the sale.

This lag in receiving cash for sales is normally the single biggest timing difference between projected earnings and projected cash flow. You will need to make an assumption regarding your billing and collection practices to determine the length of lag you need to use in calculating cash flow from sales. Typically, you would assume that sales in a particular month are billed at the end of that month and received in the next month. (To be extra conservative, you could assume payment in the second month following the sale.)

Let us assume you chose a 60-day lag (payment in the second month following the sale). Let us also assume that your sales projections for the first six months are $10,000, $15,000, $20,000, $25,000, $20,000, and $20,000, respectively. In the first month, your earnings projection will show sales of $10,000, but your cash flow projection will show zero. In the second month, earnings projections show sales of $15,000, while the cash flow projections still show zero. You can see how this can be significant. In the third month, your earnings projections show sales of $20,000, and your cash flow finally comes through with the $10,000 from the first month. The conversion techniques remain the same for subsequent months.

A more complicated timing difference concerns inventory. Typically, your inventory will cover your sales for the next three or four months. So it appears on your accrual books when you receive it, as much as four months before you sell it. But you will normally not pay your bills for at least 30 days (one month), so the timing difference is only three months, not four months. Remember, the cost appears prior to the sale. Inventory is another cash requirement before you make a sale, increasing the total amount you need from investors.

There are some timing differences that work in your

favor. Depreciation, for instance, is the amortization of the amount of money you initially spent on capital additions over the useful life of those additions. In a cash flow projection, depreciation is always added back to projected earnings (unless depreciation is not included in your projected earnings, which would be highly unusual).

Whether or not you include a particular timing difference in your cash flow projections depends on the complexity of accurate calculations of the timing difference, the magnitude of the amounts involved, and the length of time between the accrual and the payment. A small amount with a short delay can often be ignored.

Additionally, if the timing difference works in your favor, you will often ignore the effect, letting the timing difference act as a "cushion" against unforeseen future cash needs. A timing difference often used in this manner is the lag between the time your employees earn their pay and the time you pay them. This is usually at least a week, and is sometimes two weeks or more.

The format of the cash flow projections consists of two parts: **sources of cash** and **uses of cash**. The first part, sources of cash, starts with the net earnings directly from the projected results of operations, period by period. In order to convert net earnings into cash flow, you will add or subtract the timing differences for sales, inventory, etc. You will then add back depreciation, which also comes from the projected results of operations. Following depreciation, other timing differences will be included in descending order of magnitude or frequency of appearance. Except for depreciation, which is always added to net earnings, the timing differences can add to or subtract from the net earnings amount to produce cash flow. You must be careful that you are recording the effect of each timing difference correctly.

This total, net earnings adjusted by the effects of all the timing differences from operational items such as receivables and payables, is called **cash flow from operations**. It is very important—your project must have positive cash flow from operations over the long run. The prospect for future profits is the factor that induces investors to make loans and equity investments to your project. The farther into the future that positive cash flow from operations begins, the smaller the chances that you will find investors willing to gamble on your project, and, in fact, the smaller the chances that your project will actually survive, even with financing.

After determining cash flow from operations, you will show **other sources of cash**. These sources include any **loans** and **equity investments** from your investors or yourself, any funds from the **sale of assets**. You might also get loans from the manufacturers of the equipment you are purchasing, have the funds for your leasehold improvements advanced by your landlord, or use some other method to raise cash. Such sources will be listed in descending order of magnitude, and each will be included in your narrative discussion of the assumptions for cash flow. The discussion will cover such items as interest rates and repayment terms for loans, equity percentages given up through the sale of stock, etc.

Adding cash flow from operations to sources of cash from outside the project provides **total sources of cash**.

Next, you will show the **uses of cash**. In most cases, the first use of cash is **capital additions**, or the purchase of the assets and equipment used in your project. This will normally be by far your largest single use of cash. You will discuss briefly the items to be purchased and, since this schedule shows cash flow over time—again, five years—the timing of the uses of cash.

The next most common use of cash is **working capital**—the establishment of beginning cash balances and inventories. Some projects need a large beginning inventory, while others do not. In the assumptions you should discuss the requirements for beginning inventory as they relate to your project. Note that period-to-period changes in working capital are shown in the calculation of cash flow from operations; only the beginning balances in working capital will be shown as a separate use of cash.

Another use of cash is the **repayment of loans** you are getting as part of the investment. Your investors will need to see that their money can be repaid. (**Dividends to equity investors** can be shown here, but it does not need to be.)

If you do not show dividends, the cash flow remaining after all the uses of cash have been covered is assumed to be available for dividend payments. That you will have cash left over for dividends is one of the facts you are demonstrating with this schedule.

There are many other possible uses of cash. You may need to pay off existing loans, repurchase stock, pay fees as appropriate, etc. Such items should be listed by amount and period. A discussion of the pertinent factors relating to each of these items will be included in the assumptions. If there are other uses of cash not specifically mentioned here that fit into your project, they should be listed by period at this time.

Adding all the uses of cash gives us **total uses of cash** by period. Deducting the total uses of cash from the total sources of cash gives us the **net cash flow** by period. A negative net cash flow means you do not have enough cash to carry your project for the period, and you must obtain money in order to survive. A positive net cash flow means that your project has sufficient cash to carry on operations and, presumably, to pay dividends in adequate amounts to your investors. If that is true, you have a leg up on obtaining funding for your project.

Balance Sheet

In addition to the results of operations and cash flow projections, you will need to prepare a projected balance sheet for your project. The balance sheet projections will cover the same five-year period as your projected results of operations, but it is not critical that it be prepared on a monthly basis. Yearly projections of the balance sheet are usually adequate.

The balance sheet provides a "picture" of the financial condition of a business or project as of a certain date. If your project will be part of an existing business, there will be a beginning balance sheet, upon which you can build the projections. If your project stands alone, starting from scratch, then the beginning balance sheet will show cash and investment only.

As you build your balance sheet for the periods of your projection, starting with the initial investment and including all the projected results of operations and cash flow, you will show how your project will look at each respective balance sheet date. At first, you can expect your project to have large debt in relation to equity and cash balances will probably be lower compared to current liabilities than would be expected for a mature business. As the periods progress, however, you should find your projected balance sheet looking more and more "normal." Debt should be reduced compared to equity, and cash and current liabilities should become more nearly equal.

The preparation of the projected balance sheet is fairly complicated without a good grounding in basic accounting. Thus, you should seriously consider using an outside consultant to prepare it for you unless you are an accountant. The projected balance sheet is useful because it combines the results and effects of all the other projections: results of operations; capital requirements; and cash flow.

The assumptions and research you used to prepare the other schedules will remain the same for the balance sheet. The numbers found on your balance sheet must be the same as on your other schedules (as applicable) or your potential investors will lose confidence in your projections.

Even though you may not choose to prepare your own projected balance sheet for your proposal, you should be able to determine whether or not your consultant is doing a good job. The following discussion is intended to give you enough of an overview of the factors that make up your balance sheet that you can make such a determination. We will discuss the balance sheet captions in the order in which they usually appear.

The first half of the balance sheet is **assets**, and the first category is **current assets**. Within current assets, the major elements are **cash, marketable securities, accounts receivable, notes receivable, inventory,** and **prepaid expenses**. The amount shown as cash is the amount of money the project has on hand or in the bank. The beginning balance for cash (in the case of a start-up project, the beginning balance is the amount of money you receive from investors) is decreased as you spend money to purchase the capital requirements, increased as customers pay their bills to you, and decreased as you pay your vendors' bills, repay any amounts borrowed from lenders, and pay dividends. Marketable securities are short-term investments to earn interest or capital gains on your excess cash. The balance in marketable securities is normally combined with cash to determine the funds available to run the project.

If you pay your vendors' bills before your customers pay you, cash can decrease even though you are showing a net profit on your income statements. The difference between cash and profits will be in accounts receivable. Accounts receivable increase as you sell products or services to your customers and decrease as your customers pay you. In general, you prefer to have accounts receivable be no greater than one-twelfth of your annual sales (one month's or 30 days' aging), but, in reality, it is common to have an accounts receivable balance closer to two months' or 60 days' aging.

If you are doing a month-by-month balance sheet, the balance in accounts receivable would be the sales for the last two months, increasing or decreasing as sales increased or decreased in the prior two months.

Inventories will usually be the amount of materials, supplies and finished products (as applicable) necessary to cover cost of goods sold for the next three or four months. This balance will increase or decrease as the cost of goods sold increases or decreases in the projections for the next three or four months.

In some instances, you will have to pay for certain items, like insurance, before you use them. This reduces cash and creates a prepaid expense on your balance sheet. As you transfer the expense in your expense statements, the prepaid expense will be reduced. As a practical matter, prepaid expenses are usually immaterial to the total balance sheet and income statement, and they are not always shown on a projected balance sheet.

After the current assets category, the balance sheet lists **fixed assets**, which are sometimes called **property, plant, and equipment**. The individual elements often found within this category include **land, buildings, machinery and equipment, automobiles**, and **other** (roads, parking lots, utility lines, etc.). Net fixed assets increase as capital purchases are made and decrease as assets are retired and as depreciation is charged each period. **Accumulated depreciation** is deducted from **total fixed assets** to produce **net fixed assets**.

After fixed assets on the balance sheet comes **other assets** (if applicable). Other assets are those assets with a useful life greater than one year, but which are not part of fixed assets. They include **patents, trademarks, goodwill, organization costs**, etc. Other assets increase as the applicable assets are paid for or accrued and decrease as they are amortized, usually over many years. (For example, goodwill is amortized over 40 years.)

Adding up the balances in current assets, fixed assets and other assets gives you **total assets**, the first half of your balance sheet.

The second half of the balance sheet is composed of **liabilities** and **equity**. The first category on this side of the balance sheet is **current liabilities**. Current liabilities are all the debts you have that are payable within one year. The elements in this category include: **accounts payable, accrued liabilities, notes payable**, and **current portion of long-term debt**.

Accounts payable are the amounts owed for goods and services used in the course of business or construction. Accounts payable increase as you receive goods and services and decrease when you pay for them. For purposes of your projected balance sheet, the lag between receipt and payment is deemed to be 30 days or one month. If the lag is any longer, you will begin to have problems with your suppliers and your investors will notice. Thus, if you receive goods and services in the amount of $100,000 during the month and do not pay for them until the following month, your accounts payable balance at the end of the month will be $100,000. If in the following month you receive $50,000 in goods and services and pay off the prior month's balance, your accounts payable balance will be $50,000.

For our purposes here, you will assume that additions to accounts payable for any month will be equal to the amount of construction and asset purchases (inventory, machinery, etc.) received in that month and that the amounts are expensed on your income statement for that month. The reductions in accounts payable for that month will equal the amounts paid in the month, which will usually be the balance in accounts payable for the prior month. If the period you are projecting is a year, rather than a month, the balance in accounts payable will be only the amount representing items received in the last month of the year. Your consultant can figure it out.

The second element, accrued liabilities, is similar to accounts payable in that it represents amounts you owe for goods and services used during the period, except that you have not yet been billed for them. This element can include utility bills, rent, the last payroll period's wages, etc. The mechanics of increase and decrease are identical to those affecting accounts payable. One item included herein can sometimes be so large that it has its own title—**income taxes payable**. The amount in this element is the cumulative amount of quarterly income taxes payable from January until December of the year. The amount will grow for three months and be paid in the fourth month throughout the year.

The next element is notes payable, which contains short-term debt owed to banks or others. It increases when you borrow more short-term money and decreases when you pay off the debt.

Current Portion of long-term debt, the last element in current liabilities, is that portion of your long-term debt which is due to be paid in the next 12 months. It represents the principal portion of the payments only, so the amount will be smaller than the total of the next 12 months' payments, which also include interest on the debt.

There may be other current liabilities unique to your project. If so, they will be placed at this point in the balance sheet.

The next category of liabilities is **long-term debt**. This is the amount your project owes which is payable more than 12 months from the date of the balance sheet. Long-term debt is reduced when you make payments, or when amounts are transferred to current portion of long-term debt, and it is increased by the balance of any new long-term loans made during the year.

Some balance sheets have a **total liabilities** line at this point. If it is used, it is calculated by adding total current liabilities and long-term debt.

The last category on the balance sheet is the equity category. This can be referred to as **stockholders' equity**, **owners' equity**, **partnership interests**, or **proprietorship interests**. There are two basic types of equity: **investment** and **retained earnings**. In a corporation, investment consists of **capital stock** and **capital in excess of par value**. These are legal terms relating to the value per share of stock you have set in your corporation charter with the state. It is the amount you and your investors have contributed in cash or assets to the project, less any amounts that have been classified as loans. In a partnership or other type of organization, the stock accounts will not be present, but the investment has the same meaning in total. These accounts usually remain fixed after the initial investment, but will increase if additional equity is sold. The investment accounts do not normally decrease.

Retained earnings is the amount of profits earned by your project that have not been distributed to you or your investors as dividends or partnership distributions. It increases or decreases (sometimes it is a negative number if losses or dividends exceed profits) by the amount of net earnings from your project that are not distributed to you and your investors.

There may be other equity accounts, such as **treasury stock**, but we will not concern ourselves with them, since they are fairly rare.

Adding current liabilities, long-term debt and equity produces **total liabilities and equity**, the second half of the balance sheet. Total liabilities and equity must equal total assets.

The projected balance sheet and assumptions ends the financial projections section of your proposal. If I have confused you by describing the financial projections so briefly, I direct you to the sample financing proposals in the Appendix for examples of what the financial projections section of a financing proposal should look like.

CONFLICTS OF INTEREST, FEES, AND RISKS

Your proposal is almost complete, but you still have to tell your potential investors how you fit into the picture. What services will you perform besides managing your project? Do you get a fee for those services? What level of compensation have you assumed for yourself? Are your relatives involved? Do you have any conflicts of interest, where you could benefit from the activities of your project in ways other than salary and bonus? Investors expect to know these things before they invest.

Every project has at least one conflict of interest from the investors' point of view: you benefit greatly from the funding of your project. Investors know this, and realize that your financing proposal may not be totally objective. That is why you have to give your investors facts they can verify to substantiate your projections and analyses, and why it is a good idea to use outside consultants to prepare your financing proposal. Another conflict of interest common to most projects is that you will handle the disbursements for the project, including paying yourself. These conflicts of interest are not unusual and for the most part investors are not disturbed by them.

There are, however, other conflicts of interest that are not so common, and which need to be disclosed to any potential investor. For instance, you might be the sole source of supply of your project's raw materials, perhaps without competitive bidding. Most investors will let you supply the materials, but will insist on competitive bids for pricing. Or you might be selling a building or other assets to your project. How do you establish an objective price? You must disclose

the facts and negotiate with your investors on how to determine the price. Or you might be purchasing real estate for
your project, receiving a fee from the project for assisting in
the purchase, while at the same time receiving a commission
from the seller for selling the real estate. Again, disclosure
is required. Perhaps you are seeking financing for your
project and you already have three similar operations. Are
you in effect competing with yourself? Disclose it.

Although conflicts of interest are not necessarily bad,
most of them would not be tolerated in a publicly-held
company and some of them, if not adequately disclosed in
your financing proposal, could be the basis of lawsuits by
your investors or other interested parties. It is important that
any and all potential conflicts of interest with respect to your
project be clearly identified and fully described in your
financing proposal. Most investors do not have major
problems with conflicts of interest as long as they are
reasonable and have been discussed beforehand in your
financing proposal. Conflicts of interest that are discovered
after the fact can lead to the dissolution of your project. You
should consider discussing any conflicts you might have
with an attorney before you complete your financing proposal.

One potential conflict, your compensation, will be
separately discussed. You will find that this is one of the
most-read parts of your proposal. Everyone, whether or not
they have any interest in investing in your project, wants to
know how much you are going to pay yourself and what other
benefits are in your package. There are many ways to
structure your compensation. You could receive a percent of
sales, which is sometimes used in a retail project, or you
could receive a fixed salary.

Most compensation arrangements in new projects include a good base salary coupled with a bonus based on the
sales or profit performance of your project. Whatever your

compensation arrangement, you should spell it out clearly, and it should be consistent with the compensation levels of other businesses in the same industry, adjusted for the fact that you are the founder of your project. If you use a package with a reasonable base salary plus substantial performance bonuses, you will usually be within the accepted norms for compensation.

A performance bonus means you don't receive a large compensation until the project, and thus the investor, benefits. Investors do not mind so much if you benefit, as long as they benefit first. If your pay and benefits are too high, on the other hand, they will worry that your compensation is the main reason you are doing your project. Investors have the same concern about large up-front fees going to you or your partners.

The foregoing notwithstanding, it is not unheard of for a one-time fee to be paid to the developer of a project to compensate for the time and effort spent in developing the project and in securing financing for it and to reimburse for expenditures on legal and accounting work, printing, travel, etc. Such fees rarely exceed 2% or 3% of the amount raised, but if the amount raised is large, the fees can be substantial.

Lest we forget, there is a substantial risk that no one will benefit from your project. When you ask for money, you must at some point, in some fashion, clearly show that you understand that risks exist. No project is without risk. Your financing proposal is based on your financial projections, which are estimates of future events. Should those events not occur, your projections will be wrong, and your project could fail.

You may have overestimated sales by failing to understand the true market potential of your project. You may have underestimated expenses by assuming too few personnel or by making some other error in your assumptions. You may have neglected to include the effects of high inflation or high interest rates. There are any number of reasons why your projections may not occur.

The magnitude of the risk will vary, depending on many factors. How much research did you do? How far into the future are you projecting? What happens if your project misses its sales projections by 10%? 20%? If your project will survive periods where it does not achieve projected sales levels, the risk is obviously lower than if it will not survive such periods.

Analyzing the risk involves making still more assumptions concerning the effects of various conditions on your project and how well your project is positioned to counter those conditions. Known risks should be individually identified, insofar as possible, so that investors can evaluate them for themselves. You must be careful in your discussion of risks to tell investors that they may lose all their money. Don't assume they know it. If you don't tell them specifically, in writing, and they do lose their money, then they may try to sue you.

For that reason, most financing proposals contain a statement, prominently displayed, similar to the following:

> "This project involves substantial risk that the
> assumptions used concerning future events are not
> correct. If such turns out to be true, it may result
> in a loss to the investor up to the entire amount
> invested in the project."

You should consult legal counsel to ensure that all aspects of risk required to be covered have been covered.

RETURN ON INVESTMENT

You've now covered everything the investor wants to know except the answers to the two basic questions: "How much do you need?" and "What do I get in return?" You will answer them in the section of your proposal concerning the return on investment.

This is obviously a very important part of your financing proposal. In it you will convince the investor that your project, given the opportunity, can provide an attractive return on invested money.

We begin with the first basic question, "How much do you need?" You have shown the amounts you need for construction in the section on capital requirements. You have shown whether or not you need money to cover operating losses and working capital in your projected results of operations and cash flow projections. You will also need money for any fees you will receive for organizing your project and any fees you may owe to brokers for raising money for you. "How much do you need?" includes all your cash needs.

You will have to make some assumptions about the means of financing. What portion of the financing will be debt? Equity? And from which entities will you be getting the funds? The lower the amount of equity used and the higher the amount of debt, the greater percentage return on the equity invested if your project makes money. But the higher the amount of debt, the greater the amount of interest your project must pay, making it harder for your project to make a profit.

As you might expect, there are rules of thumb for this. The first rule is that you use as much debt as you can get. The second rule is that "normal" debt is available only up to about 50% to 60% of the value of your project's actual assets: real estate, inventory, autos, etc. The rest of the money you need must come from your equity investors. I used the term "normal" debt above because that is the amount that you could, with the proper guarantees, expect to get from a bank.

An example of a summary of cash required and sources of funds is shown below:

SUMMARY OF CASH REQUIREMENTS

USES OF CASH	AMOUNT
CAPITAL REQUIREMENTS	$1,000,000
INITIAL WORKING CAPITAL	250,000
FIRST YEAR'S CASH	
OPERATING LOSS	300,000
BROKER'S FEE	150,000
ORGANIZATION COSTS	200,000
OWNER'S FEE	100,000
TOTAL USES OF CASH	$2,000,000

SOURCES OF CASH	AMOUNT
LOAN PROCEEDS	$ 500,000
SALE OF EQUITY	1,500,000
TOTAL SOURCES	$2,000,000

Note that your (proposed) fee is 5% of the amount raised, the broker's fee is 10% of the equity sale, and the loan is 50% of the fixed assets. (Be aware that you may not be able to get your fee. Such items are usually hotly negotiated.) This example is for illustrative purposes only. If operating losses and construction scheduling will cause cash to be needed in the second and subsequent years of your project, show the cash requirements by year, to emphasize the timing of the cash inflow. If investors can hang onto their money for a year before you need it, they can earn interest on it, thereby reducing their net investment.

If the capital needs include the purchase of an existing business, clearly show the difference between amounts spent to purchase the business and amounts spent to refurbish or add to the business. Working capital needs should be discussed by caption—cash, inventories, accounts receivable, etc. Fees must be identified by type and recipient. Loan proceeds may involve the assuming of one or more existing loans, in addition to new loans. The interest rates, terms, and lenders for all loans will be disclosed. I know you have already discussed all of these items in their respective sections, but you need to briefly outline them again here.

Now we can try to answer the investor's second basic question, "What do I get in return?" If the investment is a loan, the answer is simple. The return to the investor is the interest on the loan at the stated rate. If the investment is equity the answer is more difficult to quantify.

Calculating return on investment (R.O.I.) requires that you assume a financing structure. You have to answer several questions. How much equity will you give to your investors? Are there any tax benefits involved in the purchase (e.g., tax loss carry-forward)? What is the tax status of the investor (individual, partnership, or corporation)? What is the organizational structure of your project (limited partnership, partnership, regular corporation, S corporation, foreign, domestic, single or multiple classes of stock, etc.)? Are there any time factors involved (delayed dividends or deferred payments, etc.)? What is the percentage of the total investment which is comprised of loans? Of equity?

You must be careful when you do this, however, because if you assume a financing structure that your potential investors do not like (usually because the amount of equity you propose to sell is too low), they will simply reject your proposal. You would expect investors to say that your project would be more attractive if they could get 50% of the equity for their $500,000 or their $100,000, but they will not do it. They just reject the proposal.

Investors will almost never counter an offer they do not like. They prefer to make the first offer and have you counteroffer. You should work with your advisors on this, but a good rule of thumb on a proposed financing structure is "If in doubt, leave it out."

This is the hardest section in your financing proposal to get a handle on. There does not appear to be any one "right way" to provide the answer to the investor's second question. I've worked on proposals where our solution to the dilemma was to simply not include a proposed financing structure and not discuss the R.O.I. And then literally every person to whom we showed our proposal asked, "Where is the structure of the deal?"

We remedied the problem by including a generalized financing structure and a discussion on the investors' R.O.I. After that, everyone to whom we showed the proposal asked, "Does it have to be structured that way?" There is no way to win this battle.

Most entrepreneurs are scared to death that they will give up too much of their project. They sit and stew about how much equity to give up and then, before they have talked to any investors or consultants, will quite often include in their proposal a statement such as "The required investment is $500,000, for which the investor will receive 10% of the company," or "We are trying to raise $100,000, and we will sell up to 30% of our equity for that amount." Without even knowing anything about these projects, I can tell you that they will not obtain financing unless those sentences are removed.

Investors don't think of themselves getting only 10% of a project. Some of them don't even want to give you 10% of your own deal. The most realistic hope you have is to be able to perhaps hang on to majority ownership.

I believe the larger the amount of money you are seeking, the more likely it is that you will need to include a specific (although generalized) financing structure. When you are looking for large sums of money, you will likely be dealing for the most part with sophisticated investors— oftentimes huge companies—that have no problem telling you what they want. They will want to see what you are proposing to sell them. If you include a financing structure, be realistic in the amount (percentage) of equity you will give up. It will be hard for you to keep a gigantic piece of your pie, when you need the investors' money to cook it. I can't tell you how much you'll have to give up—each deal is different—but you will probably not be able to keep more than two-thirds.

Likewise, the smaller the investment you are seeking, the less likely you will be to include a financing structure, or even a discussion of R.O.I. For smaller investments, you will often be talking to individual investors who will simply walk away from a financing structure they don't like. The dividing line between large and small investments is fuzzy, but is probably between $250,000 and $1,000,000.

Even if investors don't want to see specific financing structures, you may feel you should show them some calculations for return on investment. If you feel there should be a discussion of R.O.I., you must calculate it yourself for two reasons: first, an investor might not do it; and second, if an investor does calculate the return, the chances of a mistake are quite high. (They won't be as familiar with your financial projections as you are, and they will invariably pull the wrong numbers to use in the calculations.)

You must keep this discussion as general as possible, however, because you will be showing the total return on the total investment. Since you will want your investors to put up most of the money, while you keep a fairly large portion of the equity, the percentage return on total equity you show here will be as much as two times or more than the percentage return on equity that your investors will ultimately end up with. You are showing investors that the return is great enough to provide a return for them and you. You must make the investors understand that they will not get to keep the total return.

This can get tricky. Investors may not want to see the

calculation of a higher return and then settle for a lower return.

If you use brokers, they can tell you, at least for their investors, how to handle this dilemma. For your other potential investors, you can either keep the discussion in general terms or eliminate it. "When in doubt, leave it out."

I feel that there should be a general discussion of R.O.I. You can prepare a financing structure assuming that your investors have the characteristics most commonly found in investors. Some common characteristics that you should assume are that your project is structured so that the revenues and expenses pass through to the investors (a limited partnership or S corporation) and that your investors are subject to the highest tax rate currently provided in the tax code. You should allocate the investment between debt and equity, with the debt portion being as high as is reasonable. In the calculation of return on equity, you will deduct interest charges on the debt portion of the investment, and deduct your compensation (if not included in expenses already) from your project's earnings, before calculating the return on the equity portion of the investment. You might also consider delaying any payments to yourself (other than salary) until your investors have received all of their investment back.

Tax effects still play a part in the calculation of effective return on equity in spite of the changes with respect to limitations on the amount of deductions that can be used from investments. Investors are still allowed to deduct expenses up to the extent of earnings on their investments. If non-cash expenses such as depreciation are sizable, they can be used to shelter some or all of the earnings of your project for your investors, and whatever deductions cannot be used in any year can be carried forward for later use. So, to the extent that depreciation and other non-cash expenses are available, they allow you to distribute cash that will not be taxed to investors, thereby increasing the effective return on their investment. You will need a tax advisor to calculate this effect as it relates to your project.

You will hear the term "cash-on-cash return" when you discuss return on investment. "Cash-on-cash return" is simply the amount of cash distributed to investors as a percent of their investment. It arises from the realization that cash flow, not earnings, is the measure of success for a project.

Once you have made all the appropriate assumptions, you will calculate the total return on the total investment, so that you can evaluate it as to its "reasonableness." "Reasonableness" in this context means the magnitude of the return in comparison to that offered by alternate investments. If the return offered by your project is not high enough to support both you and your investors, you will need to increase the return or reduce the risk, or both. You can increase the return on equity by increasing the amount financed by debt. (Your investors can loan a larger proportion of the total investment to the project and use less for equity.)

You can evaluate the risk to the investor by performing a "breakeven analysis." This analysis will show the sales volume needed to provide the gross margin dollars necessary to cover the fixed costs of your project. Sales above the breakeven point will produce a profit; sales below the breakeven point will mean a loss. If the breakeven point is shown to be substantially below your projected sales level, then the risk to your investors is fairly low, assuming your projections of sales are valid. Every project has a breakeven point, but you may need expert assistance to calculate that point for your project.

As you discuss the return to investors and the risk levels as shown by the breakeven analysis, you should keep the discussion as broad as possible. This allows each investor to fit his own needs into your picture, and it keeps you from creating a document that could be classified as an "offer" subject to the rules and regulations of Securities laws. You should also include, at the front of your proposal, on a separate page, a disclaimer similar to the following:

"THIS DOCUMENT IS A PRELIMINARY DRAFT, FOR DISCUSSION PURPOSES ONLY, AND IS NEITHER AN OFFER TO SELL, NOR A SOLICITATION TO BUY, ANY SECURITIES OF ANY KIND."

You should consult your attorney before showing your completed financing proposal to any investor.

SAMPLE FINANCING PROPOSALS

It is hard to visualize a financing proposal if you've never seen one, so I've included three examples of financing proposals in the Appendix. These samples are sketchy and are meant only to show you what a proposal might look like. As you study them you will see how you can "flesh out" each section as you prepare your own proposal. Be sure to read the first pages of the Appendix before you look at the sample proposals.

And be sure to read the next chapter on style before you begin to prepare the financing proposal for your project.

STYLING FOR DOLLARS

You know how to create a complete well written financing proposal. Now you have to sell it to an investor. As with all other selling, first you get the product, and then you design the packaging for it. The more attractive the packaging, the better your product will be received. If your financing proposal is the product, then the style of your proposal is the packaging.

The style of your financing proposal—its appearance, length, format, and organization—is every bit as important as its content. Just as you should dress up in your best suit when you meet with a potential investor, you should also "dress up" your financing proposal to meet those same investors. The first thing an investor sees concerning your project is your financing proposal. If your financing proposal is well done, it starts to create that elusive climate of credibility for your project right from the beginning.

FIRST IMPRESSIONS

You are trying to impress the investor and give him a favorable opinion of your work before he studies it. This may sound superficial and elementary, but anything which tends to give the investor confidence is valuable. When an investor receives your financing proposal, the only things noticeable are its cover and its thickness. The cover should be simple and tasteful (colors are okay; polka dots are not) and it should be bound in a professional-looking manner.

There are binding systems costing less than $5.00 per copy that look almost like hardcover book bindings. They are designed for regular 8 1/2 by 11 inch paper, so you can prepare the contents of your proposal in your own office. Your project's logo or name can be embossed on the cover of your proposal for a small additional charge. These binding systems produce an exciting-looking book—just what you want to give to a potential investor. It beats the heck out of a spiral-bound, paper-backed book in appearance, and thus in the first impression it creates.

The thickness of your financing proposal is important because it has to look big enough to be able to contain a carefully prepared, well-thought-out proposal. There are several ways to increase the thickness of your financing proposal while also providing ease of reading and better comprehension for the investor. One way is to double-space the text, using a large, traditional type style (no script fonts, please) such as Courier (see the sample financing proposals in the Appendix). Type only on one side of each page.

Another way to add length while providing additional information to your investors is to use pictures or graphics illustrating your product or your advertising campaign. You will also have a table of contents and, if appropriate, a table of illustrations. There will be blank pages at the front and the back, and you should start each section of your proposal on a new page. These suggestions may seem like cosmetic "tricks," but each also has a useful purpose of its own, improving readability or layout, as well as adding some thickness to your proposal.

You want your proposal to be fairly thick, but it must be thick with real content. If you go too far in making your proposal thick, such as indiscriminately adding extraneous pictures or graphics, old magazine or newspaper articles, etc., your efforts will be perceived as "padding," and the credibility of your proposal will suffer.

Covers and thickness will not sell your proposal by themselves, but they allow the investor to begin studying your proposal with a positive attitude. If your proposal looks shabby, torn, worn, dirty, tacky, or if it contains just a few pages, an investor is likely to begin reviewing it thinking: "What can possibly be of value to me in this thing?"

When an investor begins a review with a negative bias, it is much more difficult to establish the credibility necessary to show that your project has the potential to be a good investment. It is almost criminal to risk losing any amount of credibility because of a simple thing like the appearance of your proposal. What they say is true: "You never get a second chance to make a first impression."

STYLE AND CONTENT

Once you have "dressed up" the exterior of your proposal and impressed your investor, you must carry through with the impression you have created. Your narrative must be literate. Misspelled words or words used in the wrong context hurt your credibility. (If you can't spell, how can you run a business?) With today's computer spell-checkers there is no excuse for misspelling any word.

Your writing style should be simple and relatively informal, but not condescending. Jargon should be eliminated insofar as possible. The investor is not an expert in your industry, but he or she does want to understand your project, and jargon does not normally contribute to understanding. I have tried to write this book using the same rules, so if you use an approximation of the narrative style of this book, you will not be far off base.

LENGTH AND ORGANIZATION

The actual length of a financing proposal can vary

substantially based on the type of project and the industry in which it competes. If your project involves an industry or product/service which is generally well known, the project description may not need to be quite as lengthy as if your project involves an industry or product/service which is new or little known. On the other hand, there may be special conditions surrounding your product/service or your management that are unique (e.g., your product was made in space; your management team all have Ph.D.'s from M.I.T., etc.). These aspects should receive additional discussion, lengthening your proposal. The financial projections will be at least 10 to 15 pages long, including assumptions; longer if there are historical financial statements to show investors. The next longest sections of your financing proposal will generally be your discussions of the market for your project and your marketing strategy to penetrate that market. When all sections are included, your financing proposal should end up being between 35 and 50 pages in length. Even the sketchy sample proposals in the Appendix are almost that long.

In addition to the above-named sections of your proposal, you may want to include an Appendix, which can contain miscellaneous detail information not always included in a financing proposal. Such information might include sample advertising brochures (perhaps from competitors), pertinent newspaper articles, or extremely technical articles or other materials concerning your project.

The organization of your financing proposal will depend somewhat on the relative strengths of the various sections of your proposal. The organization for financing proposals that I prefer is:

Overview, or Executive Summary
Project Description
Market Description
Marketing Plan

Capital Requirements and Construction Schedule
Personnel
Management
Financial Projections
Conflicts of Interest, Fees, and Risks
Return on Investment

At the front of the proposal will be the Table of Contents and, if applicable, a Table of Illustrations. These tables will show the page numbers on which the section begins or the illustration appears. If you have a large financial projections section, you may also have a Table of Financial Schedules.

The above organization is only a guide. The financing proposal for your project may have a natural organization sequence somewhat different from that shown. There may be one aspect of your project which deserves more than the usual emphasis. For example, some years ago, several retired soft-drink executives, each with decades of soft-drink experience, started a project to develop and market a new cola. In their case, investors already knew the product, and already knew quite a bit about the market in general, so those discussions could be fairly brief.

The factor that set their project apart was the strength of the management and the depth of its experience in the market they were trying to enter. In their financing proposal, the Overview would have emphasized this aspect of the project, and the section on management might have been moved toward the front of the proposal. Similarly, the financing proposal for DeLorean Motor Cars would have been focused on John DeLorean's experience running the Pontiac Division and the Chevrolet Division for the General Motors Company. (Both of these proposals raised a lot of money, and DeLorean even got major involvement by a foreign government. Both projects also subsequently failed, but they caused a lot of excitement while they lasted.)

Your proposal should emphasize the strongest and most appealing aspects of your project. Part of that emphasis will be the positioning of the section discussing those aspects of your proposal. If you are unsure whether to alter the suggested order of sections, one way to help determine the answer is to prepare each of the sections separately, and try different sequences to see if any particular order appears more meaningful for your project. If you still have doubt, the sequence of sections suggested above will certainly not hurt your proposal's chances of success.

PRESENTATION OF FINANCIAL SCHEDULES

No discussion on the style of a financing proposal would be complete without discussing the style of the financial projections. Style, in this context, refers to the format of the financial schedules, their number and their content. The financial schedules and accompanying assumptions included in your financing proposal are the basis for the answers to your investor's two basic questions: "How much do you need?" and "What do I get in return?" The schedules act as confirmation to the investor that the claims and assertions you make have some basis in fact, and that if everything works out as projected, there will be an adequate return on the amount invested.

There are many factors involved in an investor's perception of the credibility of your financial projections, but none is more important than the **exact and complete agreement between all the various financial schedules included in your proposal**. All of your financial projections—results of operations, cash flow, and balance sheet—are interrelated. Numbers from each appear in or are used in the others. If those numbers are not **exactly** the same from one financial schedule to another, the credibility of your financing proposal is destroyed.

Agreement is also required between the different sections of your proposal. You have a summary of your financial projections in your Overview. The numbers summarized must be easily found in your financial section. For example, you discuss the number of personnel your project needs in the Personnel section and the payroll expense in your financial projections must reflect the same number of employees.

There will be many other areas within or without the financial section where numbers or references will be used more than once. In every such instance, there must be **complete and exact agreement** or you lose your credibility with an investor. Remember, investors are looking for any evidence of credibility or lack of credibility. It is much easier to destroy credibility than it is to build it. Just one erroneous cross-reference can destroy everything you built with the rest of your proposal. As you prepare your financing proposal, you must keep in mind the absolute necessity for complete, exact agreement between the numbers on all your financial schedules and between all sections of your proposal.

In addition to being accurate in its cross-references, your financial section must answer an investor's questions about the finances of your project. Every investor will examine your financial projections, some in more detail than others. But most investors are not trained accountants, and financial schedules that are too numerous or too detailed may confuse rather than enlighten. Also, since you are dealing with the future, the broader your picture, the greater your chances of being close to events as they actually occur. You must have enough detail to show the total picture for your project, but beyond that, greater detail in your financial statements only gives the appearance of greater accuracy.

It is fairly easy to prepare financial schedules that purport to show each individual revenue and expense item for each month for the next five years. However, by giving essentially equal weight to items of $100, and items of $1,000,000, schedules prepared in such a manner tend to trivialize the major items. The forest is lost in the trees.

The real skill involved in preparing financial projections is to be able to prepare them so that they highlight the few really important elements of your project for the investor, while still providing sufficient back-up detail to show that you have examined all the pertinent aspects of the financial performance of your project. If you prepare the financial section of your proposal in this manner, you will greatly enhance the credibility of your financial schedules, which will reflect positively on the rest of your proposal.

Your financial schedules can be as selective as necessary, if the narrative assumptions accompanying the schedules contain the rest of the information. By including the detail information in narrative form in the assumptions and not in the financial schedules themselves, you allow investors who wish to know every detail to do so, while those who only want selected details can have that, also.

I must point out here that there are some financial-type consultants who make an excellent living by preparing three-volume, two-hundred-page financing proposals, showing every financial detail of the project, month by month, for the entire five years. The first half of the first volume contains the financing proposal we have discussed above, and the remaining two and one-half volumes are made up of additional financial schedules. It is hard to imagine the amount of detailed financial information provided. This process ends up being fairly expensive (about $20,000 for a simple project), and I have not yet seen any evidence that this greater amount of financial detail provides any greater chances of obtaining financing for a project. The work is accurate, but the time and money and effort seem to be wasted.

Financial schedules have their own rules concerning style. The following are selected style guidelines you should follow in preparing financial schedules for use in your financing proposal:

1) Round all amounts except percents to the nearest thousand (dollars or units). If you happen to know an amount precisely, you can show it to the penny in the assumptions, but show it in the financial schedules rounded to the nearest thousand. Most amounts will not be known that precisely in any case, and the accuracy of your financial projections is not enhanced at all by including a few amounts that are precise to the nearest dollar. In fact, including such amounts may raise questions from investors as to how you can know so accurately the cost of items in the future.

2) In general, no revenue or expense element should be shown separately in your financial schedules unless the amount in that element is greater than 5% of the total revenues or expenses for at least one of the periods covered in your projections. Important elements that are consistently less than 5% of total revenues or expenses, although not shown separately on the financial schedules, may be discussed in the assumptions for the elements in which they are ultimately combined. Exceptions to this rule are those elements which are always of interest to investors, such as "Interest Expense" and "Depreciation," or elements unique to your project, which should be shown separately for a more complete understanding of your project.

3) Single elements that represent 40% or more of total revenues or expenses should be separated into smaller elements, if possible. If it is not possible to divide the element into smaller components, the situation should be discussed in the assumptions accompanying the element.

4) "Other Expenses" or "Miscellaneous Expenses"

will consist of the total of those expenses which
individually are less than 5% of total expenses, but the
total of this element should not be greater than 10% of
total expenses. If it is greater than 10%, the "Other" or
"Miscellaneous" element should be separated into two
or more elements. In any case, the assumptions
accompanying the "Other" or "Miscellaneous" elements
will include a list of the expenses included in the
element along with their estimated individual amounts.

5) "Other Revenues" and "Other Income" are subject
to the same rules as "Other Expenses."

6) Titles, column headings, and element names must
be consistent between the different financial schedules,
wherever appropriate. If fiscal years are used instead of
calendar years, the fiscal year-end must be clearly
noted.

7) The first two years of financial projections will be
shown by month. This calls for a 13-column schedule
which will not fit on 8 1/2 by 11 inch paper. Even
though the schedule requires double-wide paper for the
original, we want the schedule to be on one page in the
proposal for consistency. For such schedules in your
financial section, you can use either full-size copies or
copies reduced to fit on 8 1/2 by 11 inch paper. Using
double-wide paper has the advantage of keeping all
type sizes the same, somewhat improving readability of
the detail. On the other hand, using reduced size allows
the schedule to fit on regular-sized paper, although it
must be placed sideways. Usually, this question is
resolved on the basis of the legibility of the reduced type
size. If the reduction does not seriously hamper
readability, the reduction should be chosen. The main
reason is that if your proposal contains a full-size
double-wide schedule, folded to fit in your proposal,
your proposal will tend to open to that page every time.

And these double-wide schedules are never schedules that you want someone to see first.

8) When financial schedules or other schedules in your proposal are situated sideways on a sheet of paper, either as a result of reduction, as above, or because the schedule will only fit sideways on a sheet, the bottom of the schedule should be on the right hand side of your closed proposal. All schedules should read from the top of the page or from the right of the page. (See the sample proposals in the Appendix.)

9) Type style for the financial schedules should be consistent with the type style used in the text. Do not use fancy type styles, although computer types styles are acceptable if you prepared your financial schedules on a computer. The type style should not detract or draw attention from the proposal. The spacing used in the text should be continued where possible. Numbers should be presented in 12 pitch; text in 10 pitch.

TAKE THE TIME TO DO IT RIGHT

In order for your proposal to have the best possible look and style, you will need to allocate enough time in your schedule to complete it without rushing. The amount of time to prepare a complete financing proposal can vary, but you can count on at least two weeks—if you have already done most of the research and financial projections! It can easily take a month from scratch, working efficiently. The reason is that a well-written proposal does not truly take shape until about the third or fourth draft. Each major rewrite can take up to a week, and several minor revisions will still be necessary after that. You can then expect to spend a week or two in printing and binding the proposal.

You must spend the time required to prepare a proper proposal. A poorly written and sloppy-looking proposal will do little to help you sell your project. You might obtain funding for your project with such a proposal—some projects do. But there is no need to begin your search for money under the handicap of a poor financing proposal, especially when it is so simple to have a very good proposal. A good proposal is easy to prepare when the components are covered one by one, and the necessary time is taken to cover the little things.

One final note on style. It is very important that every fact you know about your project is included in your proposal, with appropriate emphasis. The overall tone of your proposal will be positive, but all negative aspects of your project must be included and fully discussed if your proposal is to be as credible as it must be. Any side agreements, pending lawsuits, contingent liabilities, or partnerships relating to the project must be fully disclosed. Such facts will come out at some time, and they could result in the termination of your project if they have not been previously covered.

DEBT OR EQUITY?

You've finished your first draft of your financing proposal. You now know the basis parameters of your project: earnings; cash flow; cash requirements; etc. Before you redraft your proposal you need to determine the type of financing you are seeking. There are many questions and, unfortunately, there are no definitive answers. Each project and each investor requires a different structure based on the anount of money needed, the type of project and the desires of the investor.

How much money should you ask for? How much money can you get? Should it be debt or equity money? What do you have to give up? We're going to examine these questions here. To begin, we'll look at the factors that determine the limits of the amounts you can raise from outside investors. In order to successfully raise money, you must know what potential investors want and what they are willing to accept, and stay within those parameters.

We also need to expand our definition of the term "outside investor." In general, an outside investor is an investor who has never heard of you or your project, but in some instances we could be talking about someone fairly close to you. In our more practical definition, an "inside investor" is anyone from whom you can obtain money simply by asking, or whose decision is based mainly on close personal knowledge of you. An "outside investor," then, would be anyone else—someone who requires a formal presentation, a written agreement, and all the other accoutrement of an arm's length transaction.

Any definition of an "outside investor" can get fuzzy, since we all know someone that others might consider one of our "insiders"—rich Uncle Joe, for instance—but who, in reality, wouldn't give us the time of day, let alone invest in our project. Everyone's circle of true insiders is different. Some owners' circles may extend to include friends and neighbors, while others' circles may not even include their own mother.

CASH FLOW

How much money can you expect to obtain from an outside investor? In order to have even a chance to be successful in asking for money, the amount of money you ask for cannot exceed the amount of money your project can support. That sounds pretty straightforward and simple, and it is. Everyone knows it. But the primary reason that entrepreneurs fail to obtain financing is still: they ask for more money than their project can realistically support.

Every project, regardless of what type it is, has an upper limit on its ability to support outside investment. This limit is determined solely by the cash flow generated by the project. Profit margins, sales volumes, return on assets, current ratios, and all the other financial indicators you can think of, are important only insofar as they work to produce cash flow for the project.

This makes sense when you analyze the situation. Investors will not invest unless they feel they can be repaid. The only thing that will repay the investor is the cash flow generated by the project. Therefore, the first thing any investor looks for is the cash flow your project can produce. If the cash flow from your project is sufficient to cover the investment required by your project, you have a chance that an investor will give you money for it. On the other hand, if the cash flow from your project is insufficient to cover the investment required by your project, you cannot expect any outside investor to give you money, regardless of any other factor or consideration. Even if your project has adequate cash flow, an outside investor may still choose not to invest in it for any number of reasons, but without the necessary cash flow, there is no chance for any investment.

"Cash flow," as used by investors, is generally defined as the net income from operations before depreciation, interest, debt service, dividends, and taxes. This amount is taken as the measure of your project's ability to repay investors. The maximum amount an outside investor will invest in your company, either as debt or as equity, is somewhere between three and six times your project's annual cash flow, as defined above.

The reason for this is shown rather graphically by the following. Assume your project is successful and has an annual cash flow of $100,000. Assume further that you require an investment of $500,000 to maintain that cash flow. To repay that investment over the next seven years (a not unreasonably short time—investors do want their money back) at a 12% annual interest rate requires $110,000 per year. Obviously, your project cannot obtain $500,000. The maximum amount that a cash flow of $100,000 can repay in seven years at a 12% interest rate is just over $450,000—four and a half times cash flow. And that's the maximum.

Usually, investors will not let you keep their money for seven years, but will want repayment in three years to five years. And the interest rate may be 2% to 4% over prime, which can result in an annual interest rate of 14% or 15% for your project. If we change our assumptions to 14% interest and a five-year payback, the maximum amount that can be supported by your project's $100,000 cash flow is about $350,000—three and a half times cash flow.

What if your project really requires $500,000? You will then have to come up with the other $150,000 yourself. And, since your project's entire cash flow for the first five years will be used to repay your outside investors, you will get no return on your own $150,000 investment until the sixth year.

"Aha!" you say. "That applies to a loan. I'm going to find an equity investor, so that I don't have to pay back the investment." Let's examine the same project as if it were an equity investment. (For purposes of this discussion, we will not consider public offerings, which are special cases and are not available to most projects needing less than $2,000,000.) We will now cover an investment concept called "cash-on-cash R.O.I." We all know that "R.O.I." means "Return On Investment," but what about "cash-on-cash R.O.I."?

"Cash-on-cash R.O.I." means that the investor expects/ requires/demands to receive cash each year equal to a predetermined percentage of the cash invested. The "cash-on-cash R.O.I." required will usually be a higher percentage than the interest rate you pay on a loan. This is because you are keeping the investor's money. The investor's risk is therefore greater, and there must be a greater reward for that greater risk. In the example above, if the investor requires a cash-on-cash return of 20%, you can obtain the $500,000 you need, and provide $100,000 per year to the investor, but you must give up 100% of the equity.

If you only give the investor 50% of your equity, the return to the investor is cut to $50,000 per year, which will only support an investment of $250,000. Furthermore, if the investor perceives a risk level requiring a higher return, perhaps 30% or 40%, the amount you can obtain is reduced commensurately. A 30% cash-on-cash rate of return would reduce the investment available to your project to $165,000 at 50% equity.

As you can see, in general, decisions regarding debt versus equity financing are not necessarily based on the probability of obtaining greater or lesser amounts of money via either form of investment. Basically, if your project will not support a loan, it will not support an equity investment either. The amount you can obtain from an outside investor depends on two factors: (1) the amount of cash flow generated by your project; and (2) the investor's perception of the risk associated with maintaining that cash flow, which, in turn, determines the reward or incentive the investor requires to compensate for the risk.

DEBT FINANCING

Debt financing has the obvious advantage of not conveying any ownership in your project to your investor. If you have a project which is a real cash generator, why give up any of the equity? Debt financing also tends to be more structured than equity financing. The forms and the laws are in place and relatively straightforward; the rights of the lender and borrower are clear and well understood. In the simplest form of debt financing, you go to the bank, sign on the dotted line, and the money is put into your account. That type of transaction works for a car loan, where the repayment comes from your own cash flow, not from cash flow generated by the car. But it will not usually work for a large project, where the repayment is supposed to come from the project itself.

We have shown that you can not expect to be able to obtain a loan of more than four or five times the cash flow from your project. Many times the lender will only lend you two or three times cash flow, with a two- or three-year repayment period, especially for a new project. So one disadvantage of debt financing is that the repayment terms resulting from the lender's perception of the risk in your project may put too great a strain on your project's cash flow. You may not get a big enough loan.

But there is another test for a loan. You not only need cash flow, but you must also have assets available for collateral. Regardless of the amount of cash flow, the maximum loan you should expect will be for an amount representing approximately 50% to 60% of the asset value of your project. This is why you will most likely use equity financing for at least some portion of your financing.

Note: You will have heard the myths of 100% (or even 110%) financing, where you can finance your entire project with other people's money. This level of financing is found only in real estate development and then only if you meet certain criteria: you must be an established real estate developer; your development must be in a proven location; the total sales price of the development at build-out must be at least twice your purchase price at current price levels; and you must have enough assets outside the project to carry it without the loan. If you do not meet those criteria (and almost no one does) such financing will not be available to you. You do need to know about these deals, however, so that you will know where the legends about such financing arise and why your project does not qualify.

There are sources of certain kinds of loans in amounts greater than 50% to 60% of asset value. If you are buying new equipment, for instance, the manufacturer will often give you financing for up to 80% of the cost of the equipment. Manufacturers will make such loans to sell equipment. Similarly, if you lease space, you can probably talk your landlord into advancing you the money for any leasehold improvements you want to make. Again, landlords will advance such amounts so that you will lease space from them.

Thus, it is possible that you will be able to obtain a loan for your project. If you obtain a loan, you must be certain that your project can meet the payment terms. You should have a safety margin of about 100%—that is, your project should be able to make the loan payments, even if the cash flow from your project is only half the amount you project. And there should be as much leeway as possible in the default provisions. This will allow you time to remedy any breach or missed payment, which will lessen the possibility that a short-term problem in cash flow could trigger foreclosure on the loan.

You want to avoid foreclosure at all costs. Lenders will tell you that they do not want to foreclose on businesses. And, in truth, they don't like to foreclose. Not only is foreclosure a lengthy process for them, but when lenders do foreclose, they usually fail to realize the full value of the mortgaged assets.

If foreclosure is a headache for the lender, however, it is a nightmare for you. Lenders only have to receive enough money at the foreclosure sale to cover the 50% to 60% of the asset value that they have loaned you. The residual value which belongs to you is not a concern to a lender at foreclosure, and you would probably realize nothing. In fact, it is quite likely that you would still owe money to the lender if your project went into foreclosure. (See also the discussion on "personal guarantees," below.)

EQUITY FINANCING

If the cash flow from your project is there, but you cannot get a large enough loan, either because the value of its assets is not great enough or your project is a start-up or is relatively new, your only recourse is some form of equity financing. Equity financing does not normally require repayment, leaving your project with enhanced cash flow. The main disadvantage of equity financing is that you give up some portion of your ownership of your project. (There are also some tax considerations, such as the double taxation of dividends, but there are ways around most of them, and they should not play a major role in your decision on whether or not to use equity financing.)

The classic form of equity financing is the sale of a

certain percentage of the ownership of your project for a certain amount of money. In the real world, however, there are almost as many types of equity financing as there are projects and investors. Most equity financing involves a combination of debt and equity. When any amount of equity is involved, the total financing is usually referred to as equity financing, even though the major part of the money might come in the form of a loan.

Whatever variation of equity financing is used for your project, there can be no deal until you and the investor have agreed on the value of the equity in your project. Agreeing on such a value can be difficult. If your cash flow/earnings projections were completely accurate, then it would be fairly simple to arrive at a mutually agreed-upon value for the equity in your project. All you would have to do is take the historic price-earnings multiple from the New York Stock Exchange (approximately 10 to 12 times earnings) and multiply that times the projected after-tax average earnings for your project to produce your project's total market value.

By comparing this total equity amount to the amount of capital required by your project, you can compute the amount of equity you would give the investor in exchange for an investment. For example, if the total market value of the equity in your project works out to $1,000,000, and the cash required by your project is $400,000, then you would give the investor 40% of the equity in your project in exchange for that amount of cash.

But you and your investor will usually not agree on a total market value computed as above. Your investor will argue that the total market value computed as above is too high: that the projected average earnings used in the calculation are too optimistic; that the earnings are too far in the future to apply such a simple percentage; that because of the risks associated with a new project, the historic price-earnings multiples are way too high; and that those risks require a higher than pro-rata share of the equity.

You, on the other hand, will argue that the same total market value is too low: that the earnings in your projections are very conservatively stated and do not reflect the true earnings potential for your project; that new projects often enjoy price-earnings multiples in excess of the historic averages; and that the "risks" referred to by the investor are significantly overstated.

Thus, you and your investor have an adversary relationship on the question of the value of equity in your project. This does not mean that your relationship is not amicable or businesslike, just that investors are trying to maximize the return on their investment, while minimizing the risk of losing their money. You, meanwhile, are trying to maximize the amount of ownership and control of your project that you will keep. (After all, it is your idea, isn't it?)

One way to resolve this potential impasse is for you and your investor to agree to value the equity in your project at some later date. In such instances, if your project turns out to be as successful as you thought—if it meets your projections at a predetermined date in the future—the investor agrees to take less equity for his or her investment. However, if your project has not lived up to your projections, you agree to give the investor additional equity based on the degree by which your project missed its goals.

THE RISK/REWARD RELATIONSHIP

If you need more money than can be justified by the current values of (1) cash flow and (2) the investor's risk/reward relationship, you must change one or the other of the factors. However, for all practical purposes, the amount of cash flow you are using to support your request for money cannot be changed significantly. It is supposedly a fact, or at least it is based on facts or valid assumptions and cannot be changed in the short run. If you can not change cash flow, then you must alter the investor's risk/reward relationship.

This relationship can not only be altered, but, unlike cash flow, the risk/reward relationship itself will vary from investor to investor. The risk/reward relationship recognizes that the greater the risk, the higher the reward required by an investor; and likewise, the smaller the risk, the smaller the reward required to entice the investor to invest. Risk and reward are not absolutes, but are perceived differently by each investor and are subject to modification.

Please note that some investors are more amenable to having their perceptions modified than others. If your potential investor is a bank, you shouldn't count on any modification. Their perceptions are engraved in stone. This is one of the frustrating aspects of dealing with banks. You keep offering more security to try to get better terms. They keep taking your additional security, but they will not give you better terms. You have the same loan and they have all the increased security. Other types of potential investors, fortunately, are not so rigid. Let us look at some of the ways the risk/reward relationship can be modified.

First, we'll try to reduce the perceived risk. One way to do this is to reduce the amount of investment. Less investment, less risk. Easy enough. All you have to do is make a higher down payment, or increase your portion of the payments. But you are going through the exercise of trying to reduce risk because you need more money—not less. You can, however, reduce the investment from a single investor without reducing your overall monies. You do this by getting additional investors, each of which will put up only a portion of the money individually.

If you get enough additional investors, you can even end up with more money than you would have had originally, and, since the risk to each investor is lower because of the lower amount at risk, the interest rate could be lower, too.

One obvious drawback to this is that it took you forever to convince one investor to invest with you, and it will probably take twice as long to convince a second investor. In addition, many investors will not consider sharing the risk in such a manner. (See the discussion on subordinated debt, below.)

Another factor that will tend to reduce perceived risk is the presence of assets that can be mortgaged to the investor. The best types of assets for this purpose are fixed assets, such as land and buildings, machinery and equipment used in manufacturing, automotive equipment, etc. Other assets that can be mortgaged include current assets such as inventories and receivables. Patents and trademarks can sometimes have a mortgageable value also.

The downside to this method of reducing the perceived risk to an investor is that you must own the assets free and clear, and the mortgage value placed on them by a lender will probably be just over half their actual market value. Then, should the conditions arise where your investor forecloses on the mortgage, you will have effectively sold your assets for half their value. All that notwithstanding, if your assets are valuable enough, they can bring about a significant reduction in the perceived risk to the investor.

Using assets you own outside your project to help guarantee the repayment of the investor's money is another way to reduce perceived risk. This is called a "personal guarantee." In this case, you put your home, your stocks and bonds, your cars, your jewelry, etc., on the line in the event the project fails. It is sometimes called "betting the farm," and it can cause many sleepless nights.

An investment or loan where you do not give your personal guarantee is referred to as "non-recourse." A non-recourse loan or investment is guaranteed by the project's assets only. Get a loan like that if you can. I will go so far as to say that if it is possible for you to get a non-recourse loan or investment, I can think of no instance where the benefits of reducing the perceived risk to the investor by personally guaranteeing the investment can offset the grief that can be caused if the personal guarantees are ever needed.

Unfortunately, however obnoxious a personal guarantee may be, you must be aware that many entrepreneurs end up making such a guarantee to secure financing for their project. In some cases, it is just not avoidable.

Another way of reducing the risk to an investor is through subordinated debt. In these cases, one or more of your current investors or lenders might be so desirous of additional investment to help reduce their own risk that, to help you secure additional investors, they will allow the new investors to have first call on the earnings or assets of your project. In doing this, they "subordinate" their claims on your project in favor of the new investor. This means the new investor's chances of being repaid in the event of trouble are better, and the risk to the new investor is thereby lessened to that extent. Of course, the investors who are willing to subordinate must be compensated for this by increasing their reward somehow. They will not subordinate for nothing.

In many cases, fortunately, the gains realized from reducing the new investor's perceived risks are greater than the losses to the project from increasing the rewards to the current investors or lenders. Subordination is most common where the current investors are insiders, or where the project is in serious trouble and needs an infusion of new investment just to survive. Survival is the ultimate incentive for subordination.

Subordination is also common in the sale of an existing business. The seller wants to sell badly enough to accept terms (in effect, loaning money to the purchaser) and agrees to subordinate his claim on the assets of the business in favor of the other investors which have provided the financing to make the down payment on the business.

You can also lower the perceived risk to your investor

by increasing the perception of the "quality" of your cash flow projections. The "quality" of your cash flow projections is the measure of the likelihood that your project will meet your projections. An increase in "quality" means an increase in the likelihood that your project will meet its projections, thus reducing the risk to the investor. Cash flow projections are considered to be of higher quality when they are backed by factual information that reflects favorably on their chances for occurring.

For instance, in an existing project, a cash flow projection that shows the project having an annual cash flow equal to its actual average cash flow over the last five years would be considered to have very high quality. History is the best indicator of quality. If the project is new, or the history is spotty, you can improve the quality of your projections by convincing the investor that there is some factor in your project that will help assure that your projections will occur.

Perceived quality can also be increased by personal knowledge. Your investor may be familiar with your industry or your management team, for instance, and is thus better able to judge that the techniques you used to prepare your projections have validity. Or, your investor may already be familiar with your specific business or products. Franchises are an example of this. Some fast-food chains are so successful that finding financing is seldom a problem, even with a new location and inexperienced ownership.

We have discussed the most common ways to reduce the investor's perceived risk. There may be others, but they would be mainly on a case-by-case basis. You need to get to know each of your investors to try to determine whether there are any other risk-reduction buttons you can push. If you cannot reduce the investor's perceived risk to a great enough extent to meet your money needs, then you must try to increase the reward so that the investor will make the additional investment your project requires.

The most obvious way for you to increase the reward to the investor is to increase the interest rate or return on the investment. However, as we have shown, if you increase those returns to your investor, your project may not be able to pay back the investment. So, you must try to find other enticements for the investor. You'll try to trade off those other enticements for a reduction in the interest rate or a lengthening of payback terms so that you can pay back a larger investment with the same cash flow. In the world of high finance and investors, such inducements are called "kickers."

"KICKERS"

"Kickers" give an investor an opportunity to gain a greater share of any appreciation in the value of your project, if it does well, than would normally have been realized. The appreciation can be in the project's asset value (especially in a real estate project) or in the project's stock price.

If part of your project involves real estate (owned, not leased), there is the opportunity for asset appreciation, which can be shared with an investor in return for a larger investment. The investor can own the land and buildings, freeing up cash for the rest of your project. The possibility of an increase in the value of the land and buildings is very real and can be very attractive to the right investor.

As long as the main purpose of your project is to provide and sell products or services, and not to realize an increase in real estate values, you shouldn't have any trouble making this trade-off. This same trade-off is frequently made in existing companies, where it is called a "sale and lease-back."

If your project has no appreciable assets, or if you are unwilling to give up asset appreciation rights, then the "kicker" must come from appreciation in ownership and ownership rights. You increase the return on a successful investment by giving investors an additional share of the ownership, which they can then exchange for cash over and above the cash return they will receive from their straight investment.

Increasing the investor's ownership or ownership rights in your project can be done in a number of ways. The most common methods involve some combination of preferred stock, stock options, warrants, "phantom stock units" and/or conversion privileges. Before we discuss the pros and cons of "kickers" in general, we will briefly define each of these methods of enhancing return to the investor.

Preferred stock is an equity investment, not a loan. However, it usually carries a percentage dividend payment, and therefore looks like a loan to an investor. Preferred stock has one advantage to a project when compared to a loan: preferred dividend payments do not **have** to be made in any year. The advantage to an investor is that such dividends must be made (and usually any arrears made up) before any common stock dividends can be made.

Investors, therefore, know that you, as the owner of the common stock, will not be taking out dividends until they have been paid their preferred stock dividends, and thus they feel that much more secure. The major problem with preferred stock is that dividends on any kind of stock are not deductible for income tax purposes, whereas interest payments are deductible. This can have quite a detrimental effect on the net cash flow of your project.

Preferred stock frequently does not have the same voting rights as common stock, so the owner of preferred stock may have more or less voice (usually less) in the project than the owner of common stock. In a few cases, preferred stock will have no voting rights at all unless certain conditions arise, such as missing dividend payments for a certain number of years. At that time, negotiated protection clauses would be triggered and the preferred stockholders might receive voting rights superior to the common stockholders, for a certain period of time, in order to protect their investment.

Stock options and warrants are other forms of increasing the return to your investor. For our purposes, stock options and warrants are the same. There are technical differences between them, but those differences are immaterial to our discussion. The holder of an option or warrant has the right to purchase a certain number of shares in the project at a predetermined price. Obviously, if the project is successful, the value of its stock will increase to reflect that success. The return to investors is thus increased to the extent that the higher stock price exceeds their option or warrant price.

Options and warrants are frequently used when the investment is a loan from the investor. Warrants for 2% to 4% of the outstanding shares are a common level in such cases. The lender, in return for receiving the opportunity to purchase stock at, or close to, the founders' price, will loan money to the project at a decent interest rate. This allows the debt service to be at a level that can be supported by the project's cash flow, while giving the lender the opportunity to participate in the success of the project through equity without the normal risks associated with an equity investment.

Another type of "kicker" is the "phantom stock unit." "Phantom stock units" act like shares of stock, but do not involve actual stock ownership. They are sometimes referred to as stock appreciation rights. They use a negotiated beginning stock price, like a stock option. The value of the "phantom stock units" is then the amount by which the current stock price exceeds the beginning stock price. That value is paid in cash at some date in the future, with no stock exchanging hands. Because no stock is purchased, the investor does not have the opportunity to take over the project. Like any other "kicker," however, this type of return enhancer could be coupled with some sort of trigger mechanism which would allow the investor to take control of the project under some agreed-upon set of circumstances.

Conversion privileges are often used as a "kicker" to enhance an investor's return. Conversion privileges usually refer to the opportunity for a lender to convert a loan into shares in the project at a negotiated price per share. The number of shares that can be obtained through this privilege will decrease as payments are made on the underlying loan. When the project succeeds, and the stock price exceeds the conversion price per share, the investor can then exchange the remaining balance of the loan for stock. The loan is eliminated from the project's liabilities, leaving more cash flow for expansion or dividend payments.

Conversion privileges can also be available for preferred stockholders. Since preferred stock has a set percentage dividend payment, the price of preferred stock does not usually increase based on the success of the project, but will vary inversely with the movement of interest rates. Projects that offer the preferred stock conversion privilege usually give their preferred shareholders the right to convert their shares of preferred stock into shares of common stock at a predetermined, negotiated ratio.

Those are the most common types of "kickers." The primary purpose of "kickers" is to give investors a chance to get a higher return on their investment than could be achieved through the investment alone. Depending on the extent of the perceived risk, you may need to escalate the reward. Perhaps to the ultimate.

The ultimate "kicker" gives the investor control of your project. In this scenario there is a negotiated set of conditions under which the investor can actually take over the operations of your project, leaving you with less (or none) of the ownership. The conditions which will trigger such a takeover will vary depending on the project and the investor, but might include conditions such as missing a certain number of loan or dividend payments, failing to reach a predetermined earnings goal, or the necessity for the investor to invest more funds.

If you use such a provision, you will want to be sure that the conditions that will trigger the takeover of your company truly represent a legitimate threat to the investor's capital. In addition, if your project is taken over, you should retain some ownership. And in no case should you ever owe additional amounts to an investor who has exercised a takeover provision. As you can imagine, it is much easier for me to warn you about the dangers of such conditions than it is for you to avoid them.

In almost all of these debates concerning the value of equity in a project, investors have the overwhelming advantage: They don't have to invest in your project; they can keep their money in U. S. Treasury bonds and make money with no risk. On the other hand, your project will not work without their money. Therefore, you can expect to meet most of your investors' terms, if you want their money. (Unless the terms and conditions are simply too onerous to accept—I have heard venture capitalists being referred to as "vulture capitalists.")

Fortunately, not all investors look at investments in the same way. Consequently, if one investor's terms are unacceptable to you, you can take your project to another investor. If you were close to an agreement with one investor, you may very well be able to find another investor who will invest on approximately the same terms. You might even find an investor who will invest on terms more favorable to you. In the process of finding one investor, you will have talked with many different investors. One or more of them may have views on your project that are close to yours. It might even be possible, in certain instances, to be able to pit one investor against another. You do have some options.

In the process of these negotiations, you will have to contend with your tendency to get anxious. Your business is your project, not negotiations. You want the talk to end and your project to begin. As it begins to look more and more like there could be a deal, you will tend to get more anxious. Your anxiety works to the benefit of the investor, because, as time goes by, you may be inclined to agree to sell the equity in your project at less than it should be worth or you may agree to a takeover provision with too low a threshold just to get the negotiations over with. Later on, when your project is successful, you may regret some of the decisions made under those conditions.

During these negotiations, therefore, it is important to have someone competent on your side. Someone who can more objectively view the process and help you avoid giving more than you must. During these times, good outside consultants who are on your side really earn their fees.

It is also necessary for you to have objectively evaluated your project with respect to its ability to cover debt payments; to meet the needs of investors by minimizing risk and maximizing return; and to be able to carry the mix of debt and equity funding you expect. The more carefully this has been done, the better the chances that your expectations are realistic. And the more realistic your expectations, the better the chances of coming close to meeting them.

FINDING AND MEETING PEOPLE WITH MONEY

SOURCES OF MONEY

As you begin your search for funding, you may be tempted to send money to one or more of the heavily advertised business services that offer lists of sources of money for sale at up to $200. One such service even offers to match your project with "the 10 venture capital firms most likely to be interested in financing your project." (That one costs about $80.)

I advise strongly against spending money in this manner. There are about 2,300 venture capital firms in the United States, and more overseas. Lists of their names, addresses, contact information and even the type of investment each one likes are available for free at your library. No list you get by mail order will give you more information or give you a better chance to find funding than the lists you can get for free.

Think about it. If somebody really knew how to get your project financed, they could sell that information to you for 3% to 5% of the amount of money you are seeking. They would not sell that information to you for $80. Or for $200. Or even for $2,000. Save your money.

Three books of such lists, that should be available at even a small public library are:

"Venture's Guide to International Venture Capital"
(United States, Canada, Europe, and Asia)
Copyright 1983, 1984, 1985 by Venture Magazine, Inc.

"Pratt's Guide to Venture Capital Sources"
Copyright 1988 by Venture Economics, Inc.

"Handbook of Business Finance & Capital Sources"
Copyright 1985 by Dileep Rao

There will be more such books in a large library. In addition, trade groups, such as The National Venture Capital Association in the Washington, D.C. area will send you a list of their members upon request. Their list is not as comprehensive as the lists in the books above, but it is still a list of people with money to invest. These lists show the amount of money each venture capitalist wants to invest (minimum and/or maximum) and the types of projects each prefers. Almost none of the firms on these lists want to invest in start-ups. Fact of life.

If your project is a start-up, you will almost certainly have to get your money from individual investors. Individual investors are not always listed in the books, or anywhere else for that matter. You will need to find the persons who screen investment opportunities for the various individual investors. Such persons are often the lawyers and tax accountants for these individuals. It will be a long and tedious process, but it is not impossible. People in the same industry as your project may know people who finance start-ups such as yours. There are also pockets of activity in venture capital. Cities with several franchise headquarters, such as Wichita, Kansas and Columbus, Ohio, fit that description. You will find a disproportionate number of individual investors is such cities.

You are going to have to search hard to find the source of money that is right for your project. The investors are out there, but they don't know about your project and you don't know where they are. It is by far the most difficult part of the process.

CONTACTING POTENTIAL INVESTORS

One way to approach potential investors is to get their business address and send them your completed financing proposal along with an introductory cover letter. (Their names and addresses are in the books.) Or you could call them first to screen out the firms who are not interested. (Their telephone numbers are also in the books.) Or you may have your financing proposal submitted to an investor by a broker or a friend.

An investor who is serious about looking at your project will want to study your financing proposal before talking with you about it. If you bring it by in person, you will have to come back after the investor has studied it. The investor will not sit down and read through your proposal while you wait. If you pressure the investor to do that, the response to your proposal will almost certainly be "No." It is almost impossible to apply any kind of pressure to investors. They have what you want, not the other way around. Keep that in mind.

You will more than likely have many copies of your financing proposal out to potential investors before you get any response. (Don't wait for a response from one investor before sending your proposal to other investors.) You do, however, want to be somewhat selective in distributing your proposal—you do not want to be in the same category as the Clearing House Sweepstakes. Using the books, you can find out beforehand whether your project fits an investor's investment criteria. If it doesn't, don't send your proposal to that investor.

When you finally get a positive response from an investor who has seen your financing proposal, you have merely completed step one in your quest for money. Now you can see why your financing proposal needs to be so well-written and complete. You don't even get to see an investor unless your proposal is interesting.

THE INTERVIEW AND PRESENTATION

After investors respond positively to your proposal, but before they give you money, they will want to see you in person. They'll want to see who's getting their money. It's something like kicking the tires on a car. You will have one chance to impress investors with your ability and your determination to make your project work. You must make your interview work for you.

During your interview, you want your investor's undivided attention. Therefore, you should not schedule your meeting during lunch, unless it will last for several hours. You should also try to have the interview in a place where there will be as few interruptions as possible. (Outside the investor's office, if possible.) Work hard to give a good first impression: nice suit; clean fingernails; hair cut and combed; etc. If you have one or two key advisors or management personnel, bring them. If you were introduced to the investor by someone, that person may want to attend. But do not bring too many people. This whole thing is really between you and your investor. Everyone else is just a "sword-bearer" or other helper.

You will have practiced your presentation several times to determine the most attractive way to position your project. You will have copies of your financing proposal available in case the investor has other people present. It is highly desirable for you to have visual aids at this presentation: architects' renderings of your facilities; ad agencies' mock-ups of your advertisements; graphic displays of your market and projected market penetration; schematics of your products (no trade secrets, however); statistics; whatever else you have that can be displayed in large format on an easel. You will have to be able to bring all these visual aids to the meeting, along with any equipment necessary to display them. You may have a videotaped presentation that explains your project, but you must not rely too heavily on it. You must talk, too. The investor wants to hear from you. You want the investor to give you money and you must prove you are capable of handling it. The investor wants to get a "feel" for you; to see that you are what you have said you are in your proposal.

You are also trying to get a "feel" for your investors. Are they the right people for you? Can you trust them to invest in your project without trying to steal it from you? (This is rarer than you think, if you are dealing with established investors, but it does happen.) Do you want them as partners? What are their other investments? How were those investments handled from the project owner's point of view? It is as critical for you to have the right investor as it is for the investor to have the right project. An investor can make your life miserable if things do not work out exactly as you projected they would.

The interview, if it goes well, is where you will begin the dialogue (tentatively at first) concerning the amount of equity you are willing to give up. You should not suggest anything. Always ask the investor to describe the deal first. Then you can make a counter offer and begin negotiating.

In some instances, you may end up with a brokerage house helping you find investors. They may invite potential individual investors from their pool of customers to seminars that you will conduct. You will make your presentation over and over to small groups of people. Again, you must look good, and your visual aids must be clear and professional-looking. The type of investor who will attend these meetings is going to buy a limited partnership unit or shares of stock, so it is not as critical that they be "right" for you, as it with a single investor.

After you have made your presentation to your potential investors, you will have to determine how hard to "push" on them to invest. If you push too hard, the answer will almost always be "No." If you don't push hard enough, the investors may figure you don't care or aren't aggressive enough. You have to "read" your investors to determine how best to make it easy for them to say "Yes."

You may have many interviews before you find your investor. As you have more interviews, your presentation will get better. You should practice before the first interview, though. That first one might be with the right investor, and it would be a shame to lose the opportunity because you didn't make a good presentation.

AFTERWORD

Congratulations. You now know what happens when you ask for money. You've seen some of the people you'll meet. You've learned some of the things to do. As you read this book you may have come across a concept or two that you did not quite understand. If so, put a paperclip on the page, and later, when you've run into the situation during your search for money, you can review it. If you go through the whole process, there should not be any part of this book that doesn't apply at some point.

Now you can go find money. You will find sources of money literally everywhere. There are lists upon lists of banks, venture capitalists, and others with money available through magazines or elsewhere in your public library. The Small Business Administration has financing plans. Many state and local governments have financing plans. If you contact enough of them, through a broker or on your own, if your project is "good" enough, and if you are willing to give up a "fair" portion of your equity or pay a "fair" interest rate, you will get the money you seek.

The catch in the above statement is that the definitions of "good" and "fair" will be made by investors—not by you, and not by an objective observer. You need to convince investors that your project meets their needs by answering their two basic questions: "How much money do you need?" and "What do I get in return?" to their satisfaction.

Your search for funding may be a long one. Some

projects take years to find financing. In addition, entrepreneurs many times have to return to their investors or find new investors for additional funds for their project. There is no "one best way" for you to find funding. Your determination and willingness to compromise will be the deciding factors.

In many ways, you may feel your search for money resembles Dorothy's trip to find the Wizard of Oz, or Alice's trip in Wonderland. You'll swear you are meeting some of the characters from those stories (the investor plays the part of the Wizard, who is so hard to find), and you'll have to put up with some of the same arbitrary actions (a banker surely plays the part of the Red Queen). You will need to keep your sense of humor, and just keep plugging away. Dorothy and Alice got to their destinations and you can, too.

There is no question that a certain amount of luck helps here. But luck is directly proportional to the amount of effort you expend. The more doors you knock on, the more opportunities you have to find financing. And if you ask every person you contact, one of them might refer you to the right investor. With your complete, well written financing proposal, you have a better chance to find your funding.

Good Luck.

APPENDIX

SAMPLE FINANCING PROPOSALS

SAMPLE FINANCING PROPOSALS

This Appendix contains three very brief sample financing proposals. Each sample proposal is for a different type of project, to highlight the differences and the similarities in the separate financing proposals.

The three types of projects are:

I. A project involving a manufactured product;

II. A project involving retail sales; and

III. A project involving a service.

You will see that even though these three proposals project similar annual sales in their first year, their sales growth, profit margins and financing needs are quite different. In spite of the major differences in these projects, their financing proposals are similar in appearance and content. The objective of this Appendix is to show you a format you can follow in preparing a financing proposal for your own project.

We have also used slightly differing formats for the financial projections, illustrating that there is no "one right way" to present the information and showing that even though there are differences, the basic information is still there. There are a couple of different ways of handling the discussion of return on equity for the investor. You will also note that certain of the situations described for some of the projects herein would not usually be found in such a project in "real life."

You'll find them because they have been disclosed. That's the point. If you are doing something, whether it is normal or unusual, discuss it. Everyone benefits from more information.

Unlike the first part of this book, these sample proposals are printed as you will create them—as if they were typed on a typewriter. Thus, except for the fact that these samples are printed on both sides of the pages, you can see what your financing proposal should look like.

The financing proposals included here are purposely sketchy. Your proposal will contain much more about the various aspects of your project. But, each of the sample proposals does contain the basic elements necessary for a complete proposal. You should review all three samples before beginning your own proposal.

NOTE: The projects, products and services described in these sample proposals are complete fabrications, as are the financial projections. They are not intended to be used in any way other than to show you what a financing proposal looks like. DO NOT USE ANY OF THE FACTS OR FINANCIAL PROJECTIONS PRESENTED HEREIN AS PART OF ANY FINANCING PROPOSAL FOR ANY PROJECT.

SAMPLE PROPOSAL I

MARVEL MANUFACTURING COMPANY

FINANCING PROPOSAL

Prepared as of October 22, 19XX

MARVEL MANUFACTURING COMPANY

TABLE OF CONTENTS

OVERVIEW

Marvel Manufacturing Company intends to manufacture and sell high quality physical fitness equipment, and distribute a coordinated line of athletic clothing. Marvel will manufacture the fitness equipment in its own facilities. The athletic clothing will be manufactured for Marvel by a local clothing manufacturer which specializes in private label products.

Marvel will sell its products under the tradename "Sweat." The products will be sold through department stores, discount stores and fitness specialty stores. Our customers are the upscale "baby boomers" and "yuppies," who are concerned about their own fitness. Marvel will reach its potential consumer with targeted advertising in specialty magazines appealing to fitness buffs, and through mass media reaching potential customers who are concerned about new trends and the trappings needed to participate in those trends.

Marvel will sell its products within its local

metropolitan area for the first two years, with
national distribution to begin in the third year.

Marvel's management team is headed by Martin
Marvel, who has spent his entire career in
marketing and retailing, including ten years with
Fernberg's Department Stores, and eight years as
a manufacturer's representative in the athletic
equipment and clothing industry. Production and
engineering will be managed by Slyde Ruhl, a
graduate of M.I.T., who has fifteen years with
Beecher Tool & Die, in the same position. The
athletic clothing will be designed by the
internationally-known clothing designer, Lawrence Lightfoot.

Marvel expects first year sales to be $1,000,000,
growing to $5,000,000 in the third year, when
national distribution of the "Sweat" lines begins.
By the fifth year, sales are projected to be
$10,000,000. Net Earnings will be negative in the
first two years, but Marvel expects to show over
$500,000 profit in the third year and exceed
$1,500,000 in earnings by the fifth year.

Marvel requires a total investment of $2,500,000. Of this amount, Marvel is seeking an investment of $1,000,000 from outside investors. Although projections indicate a loss for the first two years, Marvel expects to be able to provide a return on total equity of over 29% in the third year. Returns in the fourth and fifth year are expected to be 29% and 38%, respectively. Marvel is expected to have a market value of $8,800,000 by the end of the fifth year, a growth in equity value exceeding 46% per year.

PROJECT DESCRIPTION

Marvel Manufacturing Company was incorporated
for the purpose of manufacturing and selling high
quality physical fitness equipment and distributing a complementary line of athletic clothing.
The equipment will be manufactured in Marvel's own
facilities, while the clothing will be manufactured to Marvel's specifications by a local
clothing manufacturer which specializes in private label manufacturing.

Marvel will market its products under the
tradename, "Sweat." The equipment and clothing
will be high-quality, with mid-to-high price
points. Each separate piece of equipment and
clothing will have an appropriate name, using the
"Sweat" theme. The fitness equipment will be a
"Pump Sweat" line, playing off the jargon for
weightlifting—"pumping iron." There will be
"Sweat Bars" for lifting, "Sweat Boards" for
situps, a "Sweat Box" portable sauna, and many
other similarly-named items of equipment.

The clothing follows the motif, also. Each article of clothing will have the appropriate name: "SweatShirt;" "SweatSox;" "Sweat-T;" "Sweat Pants;" "Sweat Skirt;" "Sweat Shorts;" "Sweat Shoes;" and so on. Each piece will have the logo—three sweat droplets—embroidered on the left breast of the shirts, the right rear pocket of the pants, or the tongue of the shoes. Pictures of the product lines are included in Appendix I. [NOTE: Not included in this sample.]

Marvel will market its products through department stores, upscale and membership discount outlets, and specialty fitness stores. During the first two years, the marketing will be limited to the local metropolitan area, expanding nationally after developing production and distribution systems.

Marvel's manufacturing facilities will be located in the metropolitan area. A 10,000 square foot facility, previously used by a wire manufacturing company, has been identified for use by Marvel. There are 10 acres of space, providing ample room for employee parking and subsequent

expansion. Land and buildings will be leased, with
an option to purchase after the first five years
of the lease.   Metal-working equipment will be
purchased.

Marvel   expects   to   need   in   excess   of   90
employees by the time it reaches the fifth year
of operation.   This will make Marvel a significant force in the local labor market.

MARKET DESCRIPTION

The market for physical fitness equipment and accessories is immense and growing. It tends to be an upscale market, personified by "baby boomers" and "yuppies," who are aging and fighting to regain the slim, trim, youthful, athletic look so popular today. You see joggers and exercisers almost everywhere, many of whom are wearing designer clothes. Athletic clothing is also worn in many non-athletic venues, such as casual parties, picnics, etc.

Marvel has conducted consumer research surveys which show that the market for its products is more than adequate to allow it to meet its sales projections. In the local Standard Metropolitan Statistical Area (SMSA), there is a population of 2,654,900, of which fully 50% are 30 years of age or older. Of that 50% of the population that is mature, our research indicates that 40% are interested in physical fitness. In addition, our surveys show that each person interested in physical fitness will spend, on average, more than

$300 per year for athletic equipment and clothing.

Based on the above research, we estimate the total annual expenditures for products similar to those offered by Marvel to be in excess of $150,000,000, in the local SMSA alone. Marvel's initial sales goals represent less than one percent of the total market.

The market for physical fitness equipment and clothing tends to be somewhat seasonal, with many of the purchases being made as gifts, during Christmas, and with another "bulge" in purchasing in the summer season, when outdoor activities pick up. Our research indicates that approximately 30% of annual sales occur during the six weeks of the Christmas season, with 35% of the sales occurring between Memorial Day and Labor Day. The remaining 35% of annual sales are spread fairly evenly over the other six and one-half months.

During the first year that Marvel is in business, we expect to realize 50% of our sales during the first summer season, and the remaining 50% during the Christmas season. In the second and subsequent years, we expect the sales patterns to approximate "normal" patterns of seasonality.

Nationally, Marvel expects to concentrate on the urban areas almost exclusively. Our research shows that of the 250,000,000 people who live in the United States, approximately 65% live in urban areas with more than 1,000,000 population. A survey of selected urban areas indicates that the buying patterns established for our local SMSA are the same nationwide. Using those patterns we can estimate the total annual expenditures for products similar to those offered by Marvel to be in excess of $15,000,000,000. Marvel does not expect its sales of $10,000,000 in the fifth year to be a meaningful percentage of the total national market.

The market for physical fitness equipment has some of the characteristics of a fad, since it arose so quickly. Marvel does not think the market represents a fad, however, since it goes along with the permanent change to a much more casual lifestyle. The clothing goes with the lifestyle, and, as long as the clothes sell, the equipment sales will follow.

Our research indicates that the change in lifestyle is permanent. And the change in lifestyle involves eating habits and leisure habits, both of which tend to promote fitness. We are confident that the market for the products offered by Marvel will exist for the foreseeable future.

MARKETING STRATEGY

Marvel's marketing strategy during the first two years of operation is to concentrate its marketing and selling efforts in the immediate metropolitan area to maximize the impact of its advertising programs. Once Marvel's product lines are established, and advertising expenditures can be increased, Marvel plans to begin the marketing of its products on the national level.

Marvel will sell its products through department stores, upscale and membership discount stores and specialty fitness outlets. After the product lines are established, the possibility exists to begin a franchise operation with a chain of "Sweat Shops," which would carry Marvel's product lines exclusively.

The advertising budget for the first year is approximately 40% of projected revenues. This level of spending will serve to introduce the product lines during the initial, pre-Summer sales efforts in April, May and early June, and during the first Christmas season. Advertising expenditures at this level will cause Marvel to lose money in the first year of operation, but they are necessary to adequately introduce Marvel's products to the public. In the second year, advertising expenditures as a percent of revenues will decrease to 25%, and will decrease to a more normal 15% of sales in subsequent years.

Our advertising budget will consist of 50% for television, including production of commercials, 30% for magazine advertising, and 20% for co-operative advertising in newspapers along with the stores which carry our products. Our television commercials will feature prominent local athletes and personalities wearing and using our products. The time slots purchased will be heavily weighted for upscale viewers, with most spots shown on local news and sports shows. Spots will also be purchased on fitness shows on ESPN, along with sports shows on other cable networks. Magazine advertising will be apportioned between regional editions of upscale sports magazines, such as "Sports Illustrated," and the fitness-oriented specialty magazines, such as "Runner," "Body

Builder," etc. Money for the co-operative newspaper advertising will be allocated to the stores which carry our products based on their purchases of our products, and how they plan to feature our products in their newspaper ads.

During the first years of operation, we will also have an extensive public relations effort to gain exposure for our products. Our representatives will appear on local radio and television interview shows, and our products will be offered as prizes at local sporting events—5K and 10K "fun runs," health club contests, etc.

In addition to advertising our products, we must get them into the stores. We plan to use the considerable contacts of our founder, Martin Marvel, to gain entree into the major stores in our market, and will use a network of sales representatives to take orders and sell our products. These representatives will represent Marvel at trade shows and on local sales calls.

The use of sales representatives will hold Marvel's selling costs to the level of commissions—10%. Marvel anticipates the use of sales representatives for the near future, although as sales grow, Marvel may begin to transfer some of the selling efforts in house.

CAPITAL REQUIREMENTS AND

CONSTRUCTION SCHEDULE

Marvel will need ten manufacturing machines to begin operations. In the second year, in preparation for expanding to a national market, Marvel will add ten more machines. Again, in the fourth year, Marvel foresees the need for an additional ten machines. Additional production needs during the first five years of operation will be handled by scheduling extra shifts of workers as needed.

Each machine will cost $50,000. Marvel has a commitment from the manufacturer on the entire 30 machines to lock in the price, as long as they are purchased according to the above schedule.

Marvel intends to lease its manufacturing space. A location has been identified which was previously occupied by a wire manufacturing company, and which, therefore, requires almost no remodeling for Marvel's use. Marvel has an option to purchase this space at the end of the first five year lease term.

Marvel needs eight weeks to be in production, most of which is taken up by the lead time on the equipment. Marvel expects to begin operations in March of next year, in time to produce equipment for the summer season, based on orders taken at the January and February trade shows.

When new equipment is added, it will be placed in positions away from current manufacturing, so that operations need not be interrupted during expansion. There is adequate space for all machinery contemplated over the first five years of operation, and the space can be segregated easily to control utilities costs.

PERSONNEL

Marvel expects to begin manufacturing operations with a production force of ten machinists.
Each machinist is capable of turning out $60,000
per year in equipment for sale. In the second year,
the production force will grow to 20, and will
reach just under 70 by the fifth year.

The office and administrative staff will
consist of 5 people during the first year, plus
management. By the fifth year, this staff is
expected to number 20.

Marvel expects to use sales representatives to
sell its products, and will contract out the
manufacture of clothing. Therefore, no personnel
will be needed in those areas.

Discussions have been held with the local
Industrial Development Commission to determine
that the existing labor pool is adequate to provide
the workers required by Marvel. We have been
assured that labor is available at the prevailing

hourly rate, which is slightly lower than the national average. There is little threat of unionization in the local community.

MANAGEMENT

Marvel Manufacturing Company has assembled a management team with impressive credentials. The company was founded by Martin Marvel, who has spent his entire business career in marketing and retailing. Mr. Marvel has spent the last ten years as President of the local division of Fernberg's Department Stores, the $10 billion department store chain. Prior to that he spent eight years as a manufacturer's representative dealing in athletic clothing and equipment. Mr. Marvel is well known to the retail buyers who will purchase the "Sweat" line of products.

Production and Engineering will be managed by Mr. Slyde Ruhl. Mr. Ruhl, a graduate of M.I.T., with a degree in Production Engineering, has spent the last fifteen years as Vice President of Operations with Beecher Tool and Die, the large athletic equipment manufacturer. His experience in the design and manufacture of athletic equipment will strengthen the company's production management.

The athletic clothing will be designed by Mr. Lawrence Lightfoot, the internationally-known clothing designer. Mr. Lightfoot will not be an employee of the company, but will receive a 6% royalty on clothing sales in the first year and a 4% royalty in subsequent years.

MARVEL MANUFACTURING COMPANY
PROJECTED STATEMENTS OF PROFIT AND LOSS
FIRST FIVE YEARS
(In Thousands)

	First	Second	Third	Fourth	Fifth
Revenues:					
Clothing	$400	$1,300	$2,800	$4,000	$6,000
Equipment	600	1,200	2,200	3,500	4,000
Total Revenues	$1,000	$2,500	$5,000	$7,500	$10,000
Cost of Goods Sold					
Clothing	$160	$520	$1,120	$1,600	$2,400
Equipment	240	480	880	1,400	1,600
Total Cost of Goods Sold	$400	$1,000	$2,000	$3,000	$4,000
Gross Margin	$600	$1,500	$3,000	$4,500	$6,000
Expenses					
Sales Commissions	$100	$250	$500	$750	$1,000
Royalties (Clothing only)	24	52	112	160	240
Advertising	400	625	750	1,125	1,500
Rent	120	145	180	180	250
Utilities	26	57	75	100	125
Office Expense	6	18	24	30	36
Office Salaries	40	87	150	220	250
Admin Salaries	120	150	175	200	225
Fringe Benifits	24	36	49	63	71
Bonus	—	—	66	128	186
Travel & Entertainment	31	48	60	72	80
Interest	48	60	66	66	60
Depreciation	100	150	200	250	300
Total Expenses	$1,039	$1,678	$2,407	$3,344	$4,323
Net Profit (Loss)					
Before Taxes	$(439)	$(178)	$593	$1,156	$1,677

MARVEL MANUFACTURING COMPANY
PROJECTED STATEMENT OF PROFIT AND LOSS
FIRST YEAR
(In Thousands)

	JUL	AUG	SEP	OCT	NOV	DEC	JAN	FEB	MAR	APR	MAY	JUN	TOTAL
Revenues													
Clothing	—	—	—	$40	$100	$60	—	—	—	—	—	$200	$400
Equipment	—	—	—	60	150	90	—	—	—	—	—	300	600
Total Revenues	—	—	—	$100	$250	$150	—	—	—	—	—	$500	$1,000
Cost of Goods Sold													
Clothing	—	—	—	$16	$40	$24	—	—	—	—	—	$80	$160
Equipment	—	—	—	24	60	36	—	—	—	—	—	120	240
Total Cost of Goods Sold	—	—	—	$40	$100	$60	—	—	—	—	—	$200	$400
Gross Margin	—	—	—	$60	$150	$90	—	—	—	—	—	$300	$600
Expenses													
Sales Commission	—	—	—	$10	$25	$15	—	—	—	—	—	$50	$100
Royalties (Clothing only)	—	—	—	2	6	4	—	—	—	—	—	12	24
Advertising	—	—	—	50	75	50	$25	$25	—	—	$75	100	400
Rent	$10	$10	$10	10	10	10	10	10	$10	$10	10	10	120
Utilities	3	3	2	2	1	1	1	1	3	3	3	3	26
Office Expenses	1	—	—	—	1	—	1	—	1	1	1	—	6
Office Salaries	3	3	4	3	3	4	3	3	4	3	3	4	40
Admin Salaries	10	10	10	10	10	10	10	10	10	10	10	10	120
Fringe Benifits (15% of Office & Admin)	2	2	2	2	2	2	2	2	2	2	2	2	24
Bonus	—	—	—	—	—	—	—	—	—	—	—	—	—
Travel & Entertainment	3	5	2	2	2	2	1	3	5	—	1	5	31
Interest	4	4	4	4	4	4	4	4	4	4	4	4	48
Depreciation	8	8	9	8	8	9	8	8	9	8	8	9	100
Total Expenses	$44	$45	$43	$103	$147	$111	$65	$66	$48	$41	$117	$209	$1,039
Net Profit (Loss) Before Taxes	$(44)	$(45)	$(43)	$(43)	$3	$(21)	$(65)	$(66)	$(48)	$(41)	$(117)	$91	$(439)

MARVEL MANUFACTURING COMPANY
PROJECTED STATEMENT OF PROFIT AND LOSS
SECOND YEAR
(In Thousands)

	JUL	AUG	SEP	OCT	NOV	DEC	JAN	FEB	MAR	APR	MAY	JUN	TOTAL
Revenues													
Clothing	—	—	$50	$150	$200	$150	$100	$50	—	—	$100	$500	$1,300
Equipment	$50	$75	150	125	150	100	100	50	$50	$50	50	250	1,200
Total Revenues	$50	$75	$200	$275	$350	$250	$200	$100	$50	$50	$150	$750	$2,500
Cost of Goods Sold													
Clothing	—	—	$20	$60	$80	$60	$40	$20	—	—	$40	$200	$520
Equipment	$20	$30	60	50	60	40	40	20	$20	$20	20	100	480
Total Cost of Goods Sold	$20	$30	$80	$110	$140	$100	$80	$40	$20	$20	$60	$300	$1,000
Gross Margin	$30	$45	$120	$165	$210	$150	$120	$60	$30	$30	$90	$450	$1,500
Expenses													
Sales Commission	$5	$8	$20	$27	$35	$25	$20	$10	$5	$5	$15	$75	$250
Royalties (Clothing only)	—	—	2	6	8	6	4	2	—	—	4	20	52
Advertising	—	—	—	100	150	75	—	—	—	—	100	200	625
Rent	10	10	10	10	10	10	10	15	15	15	15	15	145
Utilities	4	4	4	4	4	3	2	2	6	6	8	10	57
Office Expenses	2	1	2	1	2	1	2	1	2	1	2	1	18
Office Salaries	4	4	5	4	4	8	8	10	10	10	10	10	87
Admin Salaries	13	12	13	12	13	12	13	12	13	12	13	12	150
Fringe Benifits (15% of Office & Admin)	3	3	3	3	3	3	3	3	3	3	3	3	36
Bonus	—	—	—	—	—	—	—	—	—	—	—	—	—
Travel & Entertainment	5	7	2	3	3	3	2	5	7	2	2	7	48
Interest	3	3	3	3	3	3	7	7	7	7	7	7	60
Depreciation	8	8	9	8	8	9	16	17	17	16	17	17	150
Total Expenses	$57	$60	$73	$181	$243	$158	$87	$84	$85	$77	$196	$377	$1,678
Net Profit (Loss) Before Taxes	$(27)	$(15)	$47	$(16)	$(33)	$8	$33	$(24)	$(55)	$(47)	$(106)	$73	$(178)

MARVEL MANUFACTURING COMPANY

PROJECTED STATEMENTS OF PROFIT AND LOSS

ASSUMPTIONS

Revenues

Clothing Revenues in the first year are projected at $400,000, concentrated in the summer and Christmas seasons. In the second year, Clothing Revenues will grow to $1,300,000 as retailers grow more aware of the "Sweat" brand name. In the third, fourth and fifth years, Clothing Revenues will continue to grow at substantial rates. Clothing Revenues are projected at $2,800,000, $4,000,000, and $6,000,000, respectively. This trend is based on the growth patterns experienced with similar clothing products in recent years.

Equipment Revenues are expected to be greater than Clothing Revenues in the first year, due to the quicker acceptance by retailers of non-fashion items. Equipment Revenues in the first year are concentrated in the summer and Christmas seasons, because the first year's primary sales efforts will be concentrated on the major trade shows for those seasons. During the second and subsequent years, sales are projected to occur throughout the year, as seasonality factors lessen. Equipment Revenue growth is not expected to be as steep as for Clothing Revenues, with projected volumes of $600,000, $1,200,000, $2,200,000, $3,500,000 and $4,000,000 in the first five years. This Revenue growth is consistent with the experience of similar products, and does not require unreasonable market penetration.

Cost of Goods Sold

Cost of Goods Sold Are assumed to be 40% for both Clothing and Equipment, equal to the cost/price relationship of similar products.

Expenses

Sales Commissions are projected at 10% of Revenues on Clothing and Equipment. Using outside Sales Representatives to sell the products at trade shows saves the normal fringe benefits (payroll taxes, insurance, vacations, etc.).

Royalties are paid monthly to Mr. Lightfoot, at 6% of Clothing Revenues in the first year and

4% of Clothing Revenues in subsequent years.

Advertising expense is planned to occur in the months during which the majority of sales occur: primarily in the summer and Christmas seasons. The amount of advertising expenditures in the first two years is based on the cost of new product introduction. In the third and subsequent years, advertising expense is planned at 15% of Revenues.

Rent for facilities starts at $10,000 per month, increasing to $15,000 when the operations expand during the second year, and to $20,000 per month when the operations expand again, in the fourth year.

Utilities are not expected to be a major expense. Utilities are projected to be less in the summer when heating is not required.

Office Expense includes postage, copiers rentals, etc.

Office Salaries are based on employment of five office personnel in the first year, increasing to ten in the second year, and growing to twenty by the end of the fourth year.

Administrative Salaries include the amounts for Mr. Marvel and Mr. Ruhl.

Fringe Benefits are calculated at 15% of the amounts shown in Office and Administrative Salaries.

Bonus is payable to Mr. Marvel and Mr. Ruhl. Bonus is calculated at 10% of pretax profit before Bonus.

Travel and Entertainment reflects the expenses involved in attending trade shows in early spring and fall, and visits to retailers.

Interest is calculated at 12% on the outstanding balance of Long-Term Debt, paid monthly. Long-Term Debt is projected to be added during the first year, second year and fourth year, as new equipment is added.

Depreciation is based on the addition of $500,000 of machinery at the beginning of the first year, and again at the middle of the second and

fourth years.   Each addition consists of ten
machines at $50,000 each.   The useful life is
assumed to be five years.   Straight line depreciation is used.

MARVEL MANUFACTURING COMPANY
STATEMENTS OF PROJECTED CASH REQUIREMENTS
FIRST FIVE YEARS
(In Thousands)

	First	Second	Third	Fourth	Fifth
Sources of Cash					
Net Profit (Loss)					
Before Taxes	$(439)	$(178)	$593	$1,156	$1,677
Add: Depreciation	100	150	200	250	300
Deduct: Income Taxes @ 34%	—	—	—	(289)	(524)
Timing Adjustments:					
Revenues	(500)	(250)	(250)	(500)	(500)
Expenses	186	152	200	240	240
Net Inventory Production					
(see note)	(20)	(80)	(100)	(50)	(50)
Cash Flow from Operation	$(673)	$(206)	$643	$807	$1,143
Loans	400	400	—	400	—
Total Sources of Cash	$(273)	$194	$643	$1,207	$1,143
Uses of Cash					
Capital Equipment	$500	$500	—	$500	—
Payback Loans	—	100	$200	200	$300
Total Uses of Cash	$500	$600	$200	$700	$300
Net Cash Requirements	$(773)	(406)	$443	$507	$843
Cumulative Cash					
Requirements	$(773)	$(1,179)	$(736)	$(229)	$614

NOTE:
Net Inventory Production

	First	Second	Third	Fourth	Fifth
Labor	$182	$392	$686	$1,015	$1,155
Fringes	26	56	98	145	165
Materials	47	100	176	261	297
Supplies	5	12	20	29	33
Total Production Cost	$260	$560	$980	$1,450	$1,650
Less: Transfer to Cost					
of Goods Sold	240	480	880	1,400	1,600
Net Inventory Production	$20	$80	$100	$50	$50

MARVEL MANUFACTURING COMPANY
STATEMENTS OF PROJECTED CASH REQUIREMENTS
FIRST YEAR
(In Thousands)

	JUL	AUG	SEP	OCT	NOV	DEC	JAN	FEB	MAR	APR	MAY	JUN	TOTAL
Sources of Cash													
Net Profit (Loss) Before Taxes	$(44)	$(45)	$(43)	$(43)	$3	$(21)	$(65)	$(66)	$(48)	$(41)	$(117)	$91	$(439)
Add Depreciation	8	8	9	8	8	9	8	8	9	8	8	9	100
Deduct Income Taxes @ 50%	–	–	–	–	–	–	–	–	–	–	–	–	–
Timing Adjustments:													
Revenues	–	–	–	(100)	(150)	100	150	–	–	–	–	(500)	(500)
Expenses	23	1	(4)	62	44	(38)	(44)	1	(20)	(5)	76	90	186
Net Inventory Production (see note)	(20)	(19)	(19)	5	38	15	(21)	(22)	(22)	(24)	(25)	94	(20)
Cash Flow from Operations	$(33)	$(55)	$(57)	$(68)	$(57)	$65	$28	$(79)	$(81)	$(62)	$(58)	$(216)	$(673)
Loans for Equipment	400	–	–	–	–	–	–	–	–	–	–	–	400
Total Sources of Cash	$367	$(55)	$(57)	$(68)	$(57)	$65	$28	$(79)	$(81)	$(62)	$(58)	$(216)	$(273)
Uses of Cash													
Capital Equipment	$500	–	–	–	–	–	–	–	–	–	–	–	$500
Payback Loans	–	–	–	–	–	–	–	–	–	–	–	–	–
Total Uses of Cash	$500	–	–	–	–	–	–	–	–	–	–	–	$500
Net Cash Requirements	$(133)	$(55)	$(57)	$(68)	$(57)	$65	$28	$(79)	$(81)	$(62)	$(58)	$(216)	$(773)
Cumulative Cash Requirements	$(133)	$(188)	$(245)	$(313)	$(370)	$(305)	$(277)	$(356)	$(437)	$(499)	$(557)	$(773)	$(773)
NOTE:													
Net Inventory Production													
Labor 70%	$14	$14	$14	$14	$15	$15	$15	$15	$16	$16	$17	$17	$182
Fringes 10%	2	2	2	2	2	2	2	2	2	2	3	3	26
Materials 18%	3	3	3	3	4	4	4	4	4	5	5	5	47
Supplies 2%	1	–	–	–	1	–	–	1	–	1	–	1	5
Total Production Cost	$20	$19	$19	$19	$22	$21	$21	$22	$22	$24	$25	$26	$260
Less Transfer to Cost of Goods Sold	–	–	–	24	60	36	–	–	–	–	–	120	240
Net Inventory Production	$20	$19	$19	$(5)	$(38)	$(15)	$21	$22	$22	$24	$25	$(94)	$20

MARVEL MANUFACTURING COMPANY
STATEMENTS OF PROJECTED CASH REQUIREMENTS
SECOND YEAR
(In Thousands)

	JUL	AUG	SEP	OCT	NOV	DEC	JAN	FEB	MAR	APR	MAY	JUN	TOTAL
Sources of Cash													
Net Profit (Loss) Before Taxes	$(27)	$(15)	$47	$(16)	$(33)	$(8)	$33	$(24)	$(55)	$(47)	$(106)	$73	$(178)
Add Depreciation	8	8	9	8	8	9	16	17	17	16	17	17	150
Deduct Income Taxes @ 50%	—	—	—	—	—	—	—	—	—	—	—	—	—
Timing Adjustments:													
Revenues	450	(25)	(125)	(75)	(75)	100	50	100	50	—	(100)	(600)	(250)
Expenses	(154)	4	10	111	61	(89)	(79)	(5)	0	(6)	117	182	152
Net Inventory Production (see note)	(10)	(10)	15	5	15	(10)	(10)	(30)	(30)	(30)	(30)	45	(80)
Cash Flow from Operations	$267	$(38)	$(44)	$33	$(24)	$2	$10	$58	$(18)	$(67)	$(102)	$(283)	$(206)
Loans for Equipment	—	—	—	—	—	—	400	—	—	—	—	—	400
Total Sources of Cash	$267	$(38)	$(44)	$33	$(24)	$2	$410	$58	$(18)	$(67)	$(102)	$(283)	$194
Uses of Cash													
Capital Equipment	—	—	—	—	—	—	$500	—	—	—	—	—	$500
Payback Loans	$100	—	—	—	—	—	—	—	—	—	—	—	100
Total Uses of Cash	$100	—	—	—	—	—	$500	—	—	—	—	—	$600
Net Cash Requirements	$167	$(38)	$(44)	$33	$(24)	$2	$(90)	$58	$(18)	$(67)	$(102)	$(283)	$(406)
Cumulative Cash Requirements	$(606)	$(644)	$(688)	$(655)	$(679)	$(677)	$(767)	$(709)	$(727)	$(794)	$(896)	$(1,179)	
NOTE:													
Net Inventory Production													
Labor 70%	$21	$28	$31	$31	$32	$35	$35	35	$35	$35	$35	$39	$392
Fringes 10%	3	4	5	4	4	5	5	5	5	5	5	6	56
Materials 18%	5	6	7	8	7	8	8	8	8	8	8	8	100
Supplies 2%	1	1	1	1	1	1	1	1	1	1	1	1	12
Total Production Cost	$30	$40	$45	$45	$45	$50	$50	$50	$50	$50	$50	$55	$560
Less Transfer to Cost of Goods Sold	20	30	60	50	60	40	40	20	20	20	20	100	480
Net Inventory Production	$10	$10	$(15)	$(5)	$(15)	$10	$10	$30	$30	$30	$30	$(45)	80

MARVEL MANUFACTURING COMPANY

PROJECTED CASH REQUIREMENTS

ASSUMPTIONS

Net Profit (Loss) before Income Taxes comes directly from the Projected Statements of Profit and Loss.

Depreciation comes from the Projected Statements of Profit and Loss.

Income Taxes, for ease of calculation are assumed to be 34% of Net Profit. Income Taxes will be due when cumulative earnings exceed the initial losses. For purposes of Cash Requirements, it is assumed that 75% of the taxes due will be paid in the year in which the profits were earned, with the remaining 25% paid in the following year.

Timing Adjustments for Revenues and Expenses are assumed to be for one month. Payment for sales made in one month will be received in the following month. Payment for expenses (other than Salaries and Depreciation) is made in the month following the month in which the expense is incurred.

Net Inventory Production is the timing adjustment reflecting the effect on cash flow of the costs of manufacturing inventory. During the first year, for example, the plant manufactures goods for sale for three months prior to the first sale. The cash required to pay for manufacturing inventory must be included in cash requirements.

The "NOTE" shows the calculation of the cost of inventory production by month. The net effect on cash by month and year is calculated by netting the transfers from inventory to Cost of Goods Sold against the cost of inventory production. Cost of Goods Sold is a non-cash item included in Net Profit (Loss) before Income Taxes.

Loans for Equipment represent the 80% of the cost of the equipment which will be financed by the manufacturer of the equipment.

Capital Equipment is the manufacturing equipment. Marvel requires three major additions to Capital Equipment: In the first month, in the middle of the second year, and in the middle of

the fourth year. Each addition is for ten machines
at $50,000 each.

Payback Loans represents the repayment of loan
principal.   Each loan will be repaid in four
installments of $100,000 on each of the four
anniversaries of the loan.

Cumulative Cash Requirements shows how much
cash is required to be invested in the company,
over and above the loans for equipment.

MARVEL MANUFACTURING COMPANY
PROJECTED BALANCE SHEETS
FIRST FIVE YEARS
(In Thousands)

ASSETS	Beginning Balance	End of Year				
		First	Second	Third	Fourth	Fifth
Current Assets						
Cash	$1,300	$527	$121	$184	$311	$654
Accounts Receivable	—	500	750	1000	1500	2000
Inventory	—	20	100	200	250	300
Total Current Assets	$1,300	$1,047	$971	$1,384	$2,061	$2,954
Property Plant & Equipment	—	$500	$1,000	$1,000	$1,500	$1,500
Less: Accumulated Depreciation	—	100	250	450	700	1,000
Net Property Plant & Equipment	—	$400	$750	$550	$800	$500
Total Assets	$1,300	$1,447	$1,721	$1,934	$2,861	$3,454
Liabilities & Stockholders' Equity						
Current Liabilities						
Accounts Payable	—	186	338	538	778	1,018
Income Taxes Payable	—	—	—	—	96	142
Current Portion of Long Term Debt	—	100	200	200	300	300
Total Current Liabilities	—	$286	$538	$738	$1,174	1,460
Long-Term Debt	—	$300	$500	$300	$400	$100
Stockholder's Equity						
Capital Stock	$130	$130	$130	$130	$130	$130
Additional Paid In Capital	1,170	1,170	1,170	1,170	1,170	1,170
Retained Earnings	—	(439)	(617)	(24)	747	1,854
Less: Dividends Paid (Cumulative)	—	—	—	(380)	(760)	(1,260)
Total Equity	$1,300	$861	$683	$896	$1,287	$1,894
Total Liabilities & Stockholders' Equity	$1,300	$1,447	$1,721	$1,934	$2,861	$3,454

MARVEL MANUFACTURING COMPANY

PROJECTED BALANCE SHEETS

ASSUMPTIONS

Cash balances begin with the initial capital contributions of $1,300,000, and are adjusted for the net cash flow and dividends paid each year.

Accounts Receivable represent the revenues recorded in the last month of each fiscal year, which will be collected in the first month of the following fiscal year.

Inventory increases by the difference between the inventory productions and the transfers to Cost of Goods Sold in each year.

Property, Plant and Equipment consists of the manufacturing equipment purchased for the company.

Accumulated Depreciation is the sum of the Depreciation Expense recorded on the Statements of Profit and Loss.

Accounts Payable consists of the expense timing adjustment for each year as reflected in the Projected Cash Requirements.

Income Taxes Payable are assumed to be 25% of the current year's total Income Tax Liability (at 34% of Net Profit before Taxes).

Current Portion of Long-Term Debt is the amount of Long-Term Debt which will be repaid during the next twelve months.

Long-Term Debt is the amount of loans for equipment due and payable more than twelve months from the balance sheet date.

Capital Stock consists of the initial purchase of stock (1,300,000 shares with a par value of $.10).

Additional Paid-In Capital consists of the remainder of the initial capital contribution of $1,300,000.

Retained Earnings is the cumulative Profit and

Loss after Taxes (assuming a 34% tax rate).

Dividends Paid are the cumulative amount of
dividends paid by the company.

CONFLICTS OF INTEREST, FEES AND RISKS

Conflicts of interest occasionally occur in business. Potential conflicts disclosed in this section will not be deemed conflicts of interest in violation of any law or statute.

Mr. Lawrence Lightfoot is the brother-in-law of Mr. Marvel. Mr. Marvel also has a 10% ownership of the company that will manufacture the athletic clothing for Marvel. Mr. Marvel does not exercise control over the manufacturing company, and the contracts for clothing manufacture will be competitively bid every year. Mr. Ruhl intends to employ his son-in-law as plant manager once operations begin. The salary will be competitive and his performance will be reviewed annually by Mr. Marvel. There are no other known conflicts of interest.

Messrs. Marvel and Ruhl will be compensated for their activities as the management of the company. Mr. Marvel has an employment agreement that calls for a base salary of $72,000 in the first year, $90,000 in the second year, $105,000 in the third

year, $120,000 in the fourth year and $135,000 in
the fifth year.   Mr. Ruhl's base salary during
those   same   years   will   be: $48,000, $60,000,
$70,000, $80,000, and $90,000.

In addition, Messrs. Marvel and Ruhl will
participate in a bonus program, receiving 10% of
the pre-tax profit of Marvel Manufacturing Company
before   deduction   of   bonus   payments.   Bonus
payments under this program are expected to be:
$0 in the first two years; $66,000 in the third
year; $128,000 in the fourth year; and $186,000
in the fifth year.   Messrs. Marvel and Ruhl will
share any bonus equally.

The company faces many risks in the normal
course of business. Some of these risks are that
the tradename will not be considered appealing or
unique by the public, or that physical fitness does
not have the market that is indicated by our
research.

Should these or other risks materialize, causing revenues or profits to be substantially less than projected, Marvel Manufacturing Company may fail, causing any investors to lose some or all of their investment.

RETURN ON INVESTMENT

Marvel Manufacturing Company is structured as a regular C Corporation. It will pay its own taxes and pay dividends to its owners. It is structured in this form so that it may more readily borrow funds for expansion without personal guarantees from its shareholders.

Marvel Manufacturing Company requires a total investment of $2,500,000 over the first five years of operations. Mr. Marvel and Mr. Ruhl will contribute $300,000, with outside investors providing $1,000,000 and equipment manufacturers providing loans of $1,200,000. The cash require- ments are:

USES OF CASH:

Purchase of Equipment	$1,500,000
Cash Balance	121,000
First Two Years' Operating Loss	
(Includes $512,000 in Working	
Capital)	879,000
TOTAL USES OF CASH	$2,500,000

```
SOURCES OF CASH:

Investment from Officers              $300,000

Loan From Equipment

   Manufacturers                     1,200,000

Investment from Investors            1,000,000

   TOTAL SOURCES OF CASH           $2,500,000
```

Marvel will have two classes of stock: Class
A voting stock and Class B non-voting stock. Cash
dividends will be paid equally on both classes of
stock, and both classes of stock will share equally
in the equity of the company.

The investment in Marvel is intended to be a
long-term investment. There are no current plans
to sell the company or to issue additional stock.
Cash dividends are projected to provide a 29%
return on total investment in the third and fourth
years, and are projected to provide a 38% return
by the fifth year. The value of Marvel at the end
of the fifth year, based on the fifth year's
projected after-tax earnings of approximately
$1,100,000, capitalized at a conservative 8 times
after-tax earnings, would be $8,800,000, a
compound growth rate of over 46% per year. When

cash dividends are added the return on investment increases significantly.

SAMPLE PROPOSAL II

RARITIES RETAILING

FINANCING PROPOSAL

Prepared as of February, 19XX

RARITIES RETAILING

TABLE OF CONTENTS

OVERVIEW

Rarities Retailing will sell antiques and unique decorative items at retail and wholesale. Rarities Retailing will operate one retail outlet, under the tradename "Antiques and Uniques."

The market for antiques has been experiencing an annual growth of 15% in volume, with prices of certain individual items increasing as much as 200% over the last five years. The founder of Rarities Retailing, Ms. Henrietta Hystyle, has extensive experience and contacts in the antiques industry.

Rarities Retailing will occupy 5,000 square feet of selling space in the most fashionable shopping mall in the area, In the third year, selling space will be doubled to 10,000 square feet.

Rarities Retailing will obtain its inventory from estate sales held in the United States, east of the Rocky Mountains. Experienced representatives will attend these estate sales to purchase items for Rarities.

Rarities Retailing expects to have sales at retail of $950,000 in the first year of operation, increasing to a projected $4,550,000 by the fifth year. Wholesale sales are expected to be $100,000 in the first year growing to $350,000 in the fifth year.

Pre-tax earnings for Rarities Retailing are projected to grow from $18,000 in the first year to $580,000 by the fifth year, providing a projected average return on total investment of approximately 46% per year, over the first five years.

PROJECT DESCRIPTION

Rarities Retailing will be engaged in retail and wholesale sales of antiques and unique decorating items. It will deal mainly in non-upholstered furniture, occasional pieces, wall hangings and paintings acquired for it by a network of experienced representatives who will attend estate sales to buy items for resale by Rarities Retailing. In addition, Rarities will trade items with other companies in the same industry.

Rarities Retailing will operate one retail location under the tradename "Antiques and Uniques." "Antiques and Uniques" will be located in the largest and most prestigious shopping mall in the area. The shopping mall is centered in the area of the city containing the greatest number of high income families. "Antiques and Uniques" will initially have 5,000 square feet of selling space, expanding to 10,000 square feet in the third year of operation. The wholesale operation will be located in warehouse space in the same facility.

The inventory for "Antiques and Uniques" will come primarily from purchases made by experienced commissioned representatives who will attend estate sales in their assigned geographic areas. Rarities Retailing will have a network of ten of these representatives, located throughout the United States east of the Rocky Mountains. The representatives will purchase items on Rarities' behalf, staying within Rarities' guidelines. After purchase, the items will be shipped to five centrally-located collection points for consolidated shipment to Rarities' retail facilities. The western United States is not included in Rarities' buying area due to freight costs.

"Antiques and Uniques" will carry antique brass beds and other brass items, antique oak tables, chairs and occasional pieces, oil paintings, wall hangings and other decorative items. It will also carry fine antiques, from the Revolutionary War period to the pre-Civil War period. Some of these items will be purchased from an antique furniture wholesale outlet located in New England. Rarities Retailing will not deal in jewelry, due to the problems of valuation and security.

MARKET DESCRIPTION

"Antiques and Uniques" will initially have 5,000 square feet of selling space in the largest and most prestigious shopping mall in the city. This shopping mall has an average annual sales per square foot of $350, which is the highest average annual sales per square foot of any shopping mall in the nation. Some of the better stores in the mall have annual sales per square foot in excess of $500. High traffic counts in a well-managed mall located in an upper income area generate these exceptional sales volumes for mall tenants. It is essential for "Antiques and Uniques" to be located in such a mall, near higher income areas, since the appeal of the merchandise carried by "Antiques and Uniques" is mainly to upper income women for use in their homes or as gifts.

The total market for antiques and decorative items has been growing at 15% per year for the last ten years. This growth is reflected in a 200% increase over the last five years in the price of most fine furniture pieces purchased at estate sales throughout the eastern United States.

Annual sales volumes at other, similar stores
in other, similar markets have experienced this
growth. One of the largest such stores, "Olde
Thyngs," has experienced a 20% average annual
growth in sales for the last six years, reaching
$4,500,000 in 1988. Another such store, "Oldies
but Goodies," located near the largest city in the
state, has grown also. A slightly smaller facility
than "Olde Thyngs," "Oldies but Goodies" reached
$3,500,000 in sales in 1988.

"Antiques and Uniques" is projected to attain
sales of $190 per square foot in its first year
of operation, climbing to $300 per square foot in
the second year, and growing at 15% per year
thereafter. These growth projections are well
within the levels enjoyed by existing businesses
in the same industry. In its third year, "Antiques
and Uniques" plans to double its selling space to
10,000 square feet.

"Antiques and Uniques" will open in July of
this year, and will therefore be able to benefit
substantially from its first Christmas season.
The sales growth in the second year will be mainly
in the summer and fall seasons. The sales growth

is expected to mature late in the second year, reflecting the high exposure provided by the location.

Wholesale sales will be made to other antique shops throughout the eastern United States, and to interior decorators and home builders in the upscale neighborhoods surrounding the mall. During the first year, wholesale sales are projected at $100,000, growing to $200,000 in the second year, and increasing at 20% per annum thereafter. The sales volume in the first year reflects the timing of orders by other stores for the Christmas season. The second year benefits fully from wholesale orders for the Christmas season.

MARKETING STRATEGY

"Antiques and Uniques," like most specialty
retail shops, will depend on the traffic in the
mall for much of its customer traffic. This mall
traffic is primarily generated by the large anchor
department stores.

However, "Antiques and Uniques" will not rely
solely on mall traffic for customers. It will
periodically use newspaper advertising during
peak seasons such as Christmas, and will often use
direct mail to reach its market. Using lists of
high income families, "Antiques and Uniques" will
target higher income women, its primary customer.
Wholesale sales will also be generated by direct
mail to interior decorators and furniture stores.
Word of mouth and the reputation of the store's
owner, Ms. Henrietta Hystyle, will also help to
increase wholesale sales.

"Antiques and Uniques" will have its Grand
Opening in July, supported by a massive direct mail
campaign to its target market, and by newspaper
and radio advertising.

But advertising is not the only marketing technique to be used. Once the customer enters "Antiques and Uniques," she will be served by a staff of well-educated, mature and knowledgeable sales people. The salespeople will be on commission and will be encouraged to develop their own repeat customers through good service and personal notification of sales and other values. Customers will be able to sip wine and eat cheese while they browse among the fine and attractive selections in the store.

Wholesale sales are expected from interior decorators and from other fine furniture stores. Deborah DeCor, the noted interior designer, has agreed to use "Antiques and Uniques" as the primary source for antiques and decorator items for her customers. Other interior decorators are expected to follow suit. Furniture stores will also be contacted directly by Ms. Hystyle.

Pricing of items for sale in "Antiques and Uniques" will be at the high end of the scale for each item. However, a broad selection of items will assure that goods will be available at all price points from $10 to $10,000.

CAPITAL REQUIREMENTS AND CONSTRUCTION

SCHEDULE

"Antiques and Uniques" needs an initial capital investment of $250,000. Of this amount $150,000 will go to furnishing the selling space and warehouse facilities. The remaining $100,000 will be used to purchase inventory for sale and to cover operating losses during the first few months of operation.

The management of the shopping mall where "Antiques and Uniques" will be located, has assured us that the space can be readied for occupancy within 30 days of signing a lease. The furnishings and fixtures to be used in the selling area and warehouse space are readily available from local vendors and acquiring it should not delay the store's opening.

Inventory purchases are subject to the availability of estate sales with the appropriate items, but historically, there have been an adequate number of such sales during the two months of each year that correspond to the 60 day period preceding the opening to assure that there will be sufficient merchandise for sale upon opening the store.

"Antiques and Uniques" will double its selling space at the beginning of the third year. It expects to be able to pay for the increased inventory and the additional fixtures and equipment needed with its cash flow and its bank line of credit.

PERSONNEL

"Antiques and Uniques" will be open from 10 A.M. to 10 P.M. seven days a week. Initially, it will employ three full-time commissioned salespeople and two salaried part-time salespeople. Wholesale sales to decorators and other furniture stores will be handled by store management.

There will be one bookkeeper/inventory control clerk/purchasing agent who will be assisted by the outside audit firm of Peat, Anderson & Waterhouse.

The persons who will fill the above positions have already been identified by store management through prior contacts in the industry.

In addition, "Antiques and Uniques" will utilize a force of ten purchasing representatives, who will attend estate sales on behalf of the store. These individuals have also been identified by store management. Purchasing representatives will be paid on a commission basis only, and will be considered independent contractors not subject to withholding and not eligible for company fringe benefits.

When the store expands, the selling force will be expanded, ultimately reaching a staff size of 20 full-time salespeople and 10 part-time salespeople. In addition, the office staff will increase to three full-time and one part-time employees. There is not expected to be any problem in locating these additional staffers.

MANAGEMENT

"Antiques and Uniques" will be managed by Ms. Henrietta Hystyle, who has 25 years experience in the antique and decorator industry. For the last ten years, Ms. Hystyle has been Vice President and General Merchandise Manager for "Olde Thyngs," the nation's largest retailer of antique furniture. Prior to that Ms. Hystyle managed the furniture and decorator departments for Fernberg's, the largest department store in the city. During those periods, she has made numerous contacts among furniture buyers and decorators. She has chosen the ten best purchasing representatives, who have all agreed to work with her, for assignment as purchasing representative for "Antiques and Uniques."

Ms. Hystyle has also made contacts with buyers from other antique stores who have indicated they will purchase items from her at wholesale.

Ms. Hystyle is a graduate of the Amos Truck School of Business at Fairto Middlin University. She was the first female graduate of this famous institution of learning.

RARITIES RETAILING
PROJECTED STATEMENTS OF PROFIT AND LOSS
FIRST FIVE YEARS
(In Thousands)

	First	Second	Third	Fourth	Fifth
Revenues:					
Retail	$950	$1,500	$3,450	$3,950	$4,550
Wholesale	100	200	240	290	350
Total Revenues	$1,050	$1,700	$3,690	$4,240	$4,900
Cost of Goods Sold					
Retail	$475	$750	$1725	$1975	$2275
Wholesale	70	140	168	203	245
Total Cost of Goods Sold	$545	$890	$1,893	$2,178	$2,520
Gross Margin	$505	$810	$1,797	$2,062	$2,380
Expenses					
Sales Commisions	$95	$150	$345	$395	$455
Fringe Benifits	22	33	68	78	88
Rent	74	119	258	297	343
Utilities	6	12	20	24	30
Telephone	12	12	25	30	36
Pack & Wrap Supplies	14	19	40	50	60
Advetising & Promotion	75	75	120	150	180
Delivery Expenses	53	85	170	200	250
Office Salaries	12	16	45	50	58
Legal & Accounting	12	15	25	30	35
Equipment Rental	12	12	20	24	30
Admin Salaries	40	52	60	72	75
Travel & Entertainment	16	22	30	36	40
Depreciation &					
Leasehold Imp.	30	30	60	60	60
Interest	8	13	28	34	36
Other	6	12	18	24	24
Total Expenses	$487	$677	$1,332	$1,554	$1,800
Income (Loss) Before Income					
Taxes	$18	$133	$465	$508	$580

RARITIES RETAILING
PROJECTED STATEMENT OF PROFIT AND LOSS
FIRST YEAR
(In Thousands)

	JUL	AUG	SEP	OCT	NOV	DEC	JAN	FEB	MAR	APR	MAY	JUN	TOTAL
Revenues:													
Retail	$50	$50	$30	$60	$80	$180	$30	$60	$60	$120	$90	$140	$950
Wholesale	–	–	5	10	10	10	–	–	10	25	10	20	100
Total Revenues	$50	$50	$35	$70	$90	$190	$30	$60	$70	$145	$100	$160	$1,050
Cost of Goods Sold:													
Retail	$25	$25	$15	$30	$40	$90	$15	$30	$30	$60	$45	$70	$475
Wholesale	–	–	3	7	7	7	–	–	7	18	7	14	70
Total Cost of Goods Sold	$25	$25	$18	$37	$47	$97	$15	$30	$37	$78	$52	$84	$545
Gross Margin	$25	$25	417	$33	$43	$93	$15	$30	$33	$67	$48	$76	$505
Expenses													
Sales Commissions	$5	$5	$3	$6	$8	$18	$3	$6	$6	$12	$9	$14	$95
Fringe Benifits	1	1	1	2	2	4	1	2	2	2	2	2	22
Rent (7%)	4	4	2	5	6	14	2	4	5	10	7	11	74
Utilities	1	1	1	1	–	1	1	1	1	1	–	1	6
Telephone	1	1	1	1	1	1	1	1	1	1	1	1	12
Pack & Wrap Supplies	1	1	1	1	1	2	1	1	1	1	1	2	14
Advertising & Promotion	20	2	2	2	10	20	–	–	2	5	5	7	75
Delivery Expense (5%)	2	2	1	4	5	10	2	3	4	7	5	8	53
Office Salaries	1	1	1	1	1	1	1	1	1	1	1	1	12
Legal & Accounting	–	–	–	–	–	–	–	–	–	–	–	12	12
Equipment Rental (office)	1	1	1	1	1	1	1	1	1	1	1	1	12
Admin Salaries	3	3	4	3	3	4	3	3	4	3	3	4	40
Travel & Entertainment	–	3	4	–	3	2	3	4	–	–	–	–	16
Depreciation & Leasehold Imp.	2	3	2	3	2	3	2	3	2	3	2	3	30
Interest	–	1	1	1	1	–	1	–	1	1	1	1	8
Other	1	–	1	–	1	–	1	–	1	–	1	–	6
Total Expenses	$42	$29	$25	$31	$42	$81	$21	$30	$31	$48	$39	$68	$487
Income (Loss) before Taxes	$(17)	$(4)	$(8)	$2	$1	$12	$(6)	$0	$2	$19	$9	$8	$18

RARITIES RETAILING

PROJECTED STATEMENT OF PROFIT AND LOSS

SECOND YEAR

(In Thousands)

	JUL	AUG	SEP	OCT	NOV	DEC	JAN	FEB	MAR	APR	MAY	JUN	TOTAL
Revenues:													
Retail	$110	$100	$90	$100	$140	$300	$50	$90	$90	$150	$120	$160	$1,500
Wholesale	—	20	40	30	30	10	—	—	10	30	20	10	200
Total Revenues	$110	$120	$130	$130	$170	$310	$50	$90	$100	$180	$140	$170	$1,700
Cost of Goods Sold:													
Retail	$55	$50	$45	$50	$70	150	$25	$45	$45	$75	$60	$80	$750
Wholesale	—	14	28	21	21	7	—	—	7	21	14	7	140
Total Cost of Goods Sold	$55	$64	$73	$71	$91	$157	$25	$45	$52	$96	$74	$87	$890
Gross Margin	$55	$56	$57	$59	$79	$153	$25	$45	$48	$84	$66	$83	$810
Expenses													
Sales Commissions	$11	$10	$9	$10	$14	$30	$5	$9	$9	$15	$12	$16	$150
Fringe Benifits	2	2	2	3	3	6	2	2	2	3	3	3	33
Rent (7%)	8	8	9	9	12	22	3	6	7	13	10	12	119
Utilities	1	1	1	1	1	1	1	1	1	1	1	1	12
Telephone	1	1	1	1	1	1	1	1	1	1	1	1	12
Pack & Wrap Supplies	1	1	1	2	2	4	—	1	2	2	2	2	19
Advertising & Promotion	2	2	2	2	10	25	—	2	5	6	6	9	75
Delivery Expense (5%)	5	6	7	8	8	15	2	5	5	9	7	8	85
Office Salaries	1	1	2	1	1	2	1	1	2	1	1	2	16
Legal & Accounting	—	—	—	—	—	—	—	—	—	—	—	15	15
Equipment Rental (office)	1	1	1	1	1	1	1	1	1	1	1	1	12
Admin Salaries	4	4	5	4	4	5	4	4	5	4	4	5	52
Travel & Entertainment	1	3	4	1	1	1	4	3	1	1	1	1	22
Depreciation & Leasehold Imp.	2	3	2	3	2	3	2	3	2	3	2	3	30
Interest	1	1	1	1	1	—	1	1	1	1	2	2	13
Other	1	1	1	1	1	1	1	1	1	1	1	1	12
Total Expenses	$42	$45	$48	$48	$62	$117	$28	$41	$49	$61	$54	$82	$677
Income (Loss) before Taxes	$13	$11	$9	$11	$17	$36	$(3)	$4	$(1)	$23	$12	$1	$133

RARITIES RETAILING

PROJECTED STATEMENTS OF PROFIT AND LOSS

ASSUMPTIONS

Revenues

Retail Revenues are based on 5,000 square feet of selling space with annual sales of $250 per square foot in the first year and $300 per square foot in the second year. In the third year, selling space is increased to 10,000 square feet, and sales per square foot increase to $345. Annual sales per square foot are assumed to increase to $395 in year four and to $455 in year five. Retail Revenues are allocated by month in accordance with normal seasonal sales patterns in the industry, with approximately 20% of annual sales occurring in December.

Retail Revenues are shown net of 5% sales taxes.

Wholesale Revenues represent sales to interior decorators and other furniture stores. They are projected to be $100,000 in the first year, increasing to $200,000 in the second year, and increasing at 20% per year thereafter.

Cost of Goods Sold

Retail Cost of Goods Sold includes purchasing commissions and freight costs to the store. It is assumed to be 50% of Retail Revenues, net of Sales Taxes.

Wholesale Cost of Goods Sold is assumed to be 70% of Wholesale Revenues, including purchasing commissions and freight costs to the store.

Expenses

Sales Commissions are paid at the rate of 10% of Retail Revenues. Sales Salaries are included, and are assumed to be approximately 10% of Retail Revenues resulting from sales by salaried personnel.

Fringe Benefits include payroll taxes, health insurance, etc. They are assumed to be 15% of Sales Commissions and Salaries. There are no fringe benefits on buying commissions.

Rent is assumed to be 7% of Revenues.

Utilities are assumed at $500 per month in the first year, increasing with inflation and store size.

Telephone expense is projected at $1,000 per month in the first year, increasing with sales and store size.

Pack and Wrap Supplies are expected to be between 1% and 1 and 1/2% of Revenues.

Advertising and Promotion includes the cost of direct mail campaigns and seasonal advertising. This expense is budgeted annually at between 3% and 5% of Revenues, except during the first year, when it is projected at 7% of revenues. First month's expenditures reflect the support for the Grand Opening of the store.

Delivery expense is assumed to be 5% of Revenues.

Office Salaries represent one office employee in the first year, with the staff growing as Revenues and store size grow.

Legal and Accounting is primarily the cost of the annual audit and periodic assistance to the office staff. It is charged as a lump sum in the last month of the year.

Equipment Rental includes the cost of copiers, ticket making machines, etc.

Administrative Salaries consists of the compensation of Ms. Hystyle, not including ownership interests.

Travel and Entertainment includes expenses for travel to gift shows and auctions, and for entertainment of wholesale customers.

Depreciation and Leasehold Improvements is based on the initial cost of $150,000 for finishing the selling space and purchasing the selling fixtures and display items. All these items are assumed to have a five year life. When the store size is doubled in year three, the cost is expected to again be $150,000, with a five year life.

Interest is assumed at 10% per year on the outstanding balance of the bank line of credit. The bank line of credit is figured at 50% of inventory at cost, plus, in year three, an equipment loan of $100,000 at 10% for five years.

RARITIES RETAILING
PROJECTED SOURCES AND USES OF CASH
FIRST FIVE YEARS
(In Thousands)

	First	Second	Third	Fourth	Fifth
SOURCES OF CASH					
Income (Loss) from Operations	$18	$133	$465	$508	$580
Add: Depreciation	30	30	60	60	60
Timing Adjustments					
for Expenses	57	13	62	20	22
Inventory Level Adjustments	(124)	(248)	(66)	(76)	(88)
Cash Flow From Operations	$(19)	$(72)	$521	$512	$574
Investment	$250	—	—	—	—
Bank Line of Credit	96	$124	$113	$18	$24
Total Sources of Cash	$327	$52	$634	$530	$598
USES OF CASH					
Capital Improvements	$150	—	$150	—	—
Beginnings Inventory	68	—	—	—	—
Dividends	30	$40	400	$500	$600
Total Uses of Cash	$248	$40	$550	$500	$600
Net Cash Flow	$79	$12	$84	$30	$(2)

RARITIES RETAILING
PROJECTED SOURCES AND USES OF CASH
FIRST YEAR
(In Thousands)

	JUL	AUG	SEP	OCT	NOV	DEC	JAN	FEB	MAR	APR	MAY	JUN	TOTAL
SOURCES OF CASH													
Income (Loss) before Taxes	$(17)	$(4)	$(8)	$2	$1	$12	$(6)	$0	$2	$19	$9	$8	$18
Add: Depreciation	2	3	2	3	2	3	2	3	2	3	2	3	30
Timing Adjustments for Expenses	36	(14)	(1)	3	11	33	(51)	6	2	13	(6)	25	57
Inventory Level Adjustment	(12)	(22)	(79)	22	7	70	(63)	(22)	(47)	23	(12)	11	(124)
Cash Flow from Operations	$9	$(37)	$(86)	$30	$21	$118	$(118)	$(13)	$(41)	$58	$(7)	$47	$(19)
Investments	$250	—	—	—	—	—	—	—	—	—	—	—	$250
Bank Line of Credit	40	11	40	(11)	(4)	(35)	31	11	24	(12)	6	(5)	96
Total Sources of Cash	$299	$(26)	$(46)	$19	$17	$83	$(87)	$(2)	$(17)	$46	$(1)	$42	$327
USES OF CASH													
Beginning Inventory	$68	—	—	—	—	—	—	—	—	—	—	—	$68
Capital Improvements	150	—	—	—	—	—	—	—	—	—	—	—	150
Dividends to Owners	—	—	—	—	—	—	—	—	—	—	—	$30	30
Total Uses of Cash	$218	—	—	—	—	—	—	—	—	—	—	$30	$248
Net Cash Flow	$81	$(26)	$(46)	$19	$17	$83	$(87)	$(2)	$(17)	$46	$(1)	$12	$79
Cumulative Cash Flow	$81	$55	$9	$28	$45	$128	$41	$39	$22	$68	$67	$79	

RARITIES RETAILING
PROJECTED SOURCES AND USES OF CASH
SECOND YEAR
(In Thousands)

	JUL	AUG	SEP	OCT	NOV	DEC	JAN	FEB	MAR	APR	MAY	JUN	TOTAL
SOURCES OF CASH													
Income (Loss) from Operations	$13	$11	$9	$11	$17	$36	$(3)	$4	$(1)	$23	$12	$1	$133
Add: Depreciation	2	3	2	3	2	3	2	3	2	3	2	3	30
Timing Adjustments													
for Expenses	(24)	3	5	(2)	13	46	(76)	11	9	7	(4)	25	13
Inventory Level Adjustment	(16)	(27)	(84)	46	46	105	(71)	(29)	(35)	(30)	(73)	(80)	(248)
Cash Flow from Operations	$(25)	$(10)	$(68)	$58	$78	$190	$(148)	$(11)	$(25)	$3	$(63)	$(51)	$(72)
Bank Line of Credit	$8	$14	$42	$(23)	$(23)	$(53)	$36	$14	$18	$15	$36	$40	$124
Total Sources of Cash	$(17)	$4	$(26)	$35	$55	$137	$(112)	$3	$(7)	$18	$(27)	$(11)	$52
USES OF CASH													
Dividends to Owners	—	—	—	—	—	—	—	—	—	—	—	$40	$40
Total Uses of Cash	—	—	—	—	—	—	—	—	—	—	—	$40	$40
Net Cash Flow	$(17)	$4	$(26)	$35	$55	$137	$(112)	$3	$(7)	$18	$(27)	$(51)	$12
Cumulative Cash Flow	$62	$66	$40	$75	$130	$267	$155	$158	$151	$169	$142	$91	

RARITIES RETAILING

PROJECTED SOURCES AND USES OF CASH

ASSUMPTIONS

Timing Adjustments

Expenses other than inventory, payroll, and depreciation are paid in the month following the month in which they appear on the profit and loss projections. This adjustment also includes Sales Taxes, paid in the month following the sales, at 5% of Retail Revenues.

Inventory Levels fluctuate, based on four turns per year, with payment for purchases as they are made. (Estate Sales are cash only.) At the end of each month, the inventory will equal the total of the Cost of Goods Sold projections for the next three months. As the projected Cost of Goods Sold change, the inventory levels will fluctuate, up or down. At the end of the second year, the inventory levels increase to allow for the increase in the size of the store.

Beginning Inventory is assumed to be purchased when the store opens. It will actually be purchased in the three months prior to store opening. The amount is the total of the first three months' projected Cost of Goods Sold.

Capital Improvements is the finish of the selling space and the purchase of selling fixtures and display items for the new store, and again when the store is expanded. Each expansion is assumed to cost $150,000.

Bank Line of Credit is equal to 50% of the inventory. As the inventory increases, the credit line increases; as the inventory decreases, the credit line is paid down proportionately. There is also a $100,000 equipment loan to help pay for the expansion of selling space in the third year. This loan is payable over five years.

RARITIES RETAILING
PROJECTED BALANCE SHEETS
AT YEAR END, FIRST FIVE YEARS
(In Thousands)

	First	Second	Third	Fourth	Fifth
ASSETS					
Current Assets					
Cash	$79	$91	$175	$205	$203
Inventory	192	440	506	582	670
Total Current Assets	$271	$531	$681	$787	$873
Leasehold Imp. & Fixtures	$150	$150	$300	$300	$300
Less Accumulated Depreciation	(30)	(60)	(120)	(180)	(240)
	$120	$90	$180	$120	$60
Total Assets	$391	$621	$861	$907	$933
LIABILITIES & PARTNERSHIP ACCOUNTS					
Current Liabilities					
Accounts Payable	$50	$62	$114	$131	$150
Sales Tax Payable	7	8	18	21	24
Notes Payable	96	220	333	351	375
Total Current Liabilities	$153	$290	$465	$503	$549
Partnership Accounts					
Contributed Capital	$250	$250	$250	$250	$250
Partnership Earnings	18	151	616	1124	1704
Less Partners' Draw	(30)	(70)	(470)	(970)	(1,570)
Total Partnership accounts	$238	$331	$396	$404	$384
Total Liabilities and Stockholders' Equity	$391	$621	$861	$907	$933

RARITIES RETAILING

PROJECTED BALANCE SHEETS

ASSUMPTIONS

Assets

Cash balance in the first year is the amount from the projected Sources and Uses of Cash. In subsequent years, the amount is adjusted by the amounts shown on the projected Sources and Uses of Cash, year by year. The amount is maintained at a level approximately equal to Current Liabilities.

Inventory balance is equal to the projected Cost of Goods Sold for the three months following the balance sheet date.

Leasehold Improvements and Fixtures contains the cost to finish the selling space and to purchase selling fixtures and display items. The balance in the first year is for the original store. The increase in the third year is for the expansion of selling space.

Accumulated Depreciation is the total of the depreciation expense recognized in the projected statements of Profit and Loss. All equipment is assumed to have a five year life.

Liabilities

Accounts Payable includes the amounts due for expenses incurred in the last month of the fiscal year, which will be paid in the first month of the next year. This amount plus Sales Taxes Payable are shown as expense timing adjustments on the projected Sources and Uses of Cash.

Sales Taxes Payable is calculated at 5% of the prior month's Retail Revenues.

Contributed Capital is the initial capital investment of $250,000.

Partnership Earnings is the cumulative earnings of the company before taxes as shown on the projected Statements of Profit and Loss.

Partners' Draws are the cumulative cash payments to the partners.

CONFLICTS OF INTEREST, FEES AND RISKS

There are two apparent conflicts of interest in Rarities Retailing.   The first is that Ms. Hystyle will herself occasionally buy items at estate sales, and she will receive a purchasing commission on such purchases. The second conflict of interest is that Ms. Hystyle owns a ten percent interest in the New England antique store from which "Antiques and Uniques" intends to purchase some of its inventory items. Ms. Hystyle does not control the New England store, nor set its prices, and does not expect to benefit unduly from her ownership position in that store.

Ms. Hystyle will receive direct compensation for her services as store management.   Such compensation will amount to $40,000 in the first year; $52,000 in the second year; $60,000 in the third year; $72,000 in the fourth year; and $75,000 in the fifth year.

Ms. Hystyle will also receive a company-paid health plan and life insurance policy and the use of a company car.

Rarities Retailing and its outlet "Antiques

and Uniques" require a large inventory of high cost merchandise. There is no guarantee that such merchandise will appeal to potential customers and the lines of supply—estate sales over a large part of the United States—may turn out to be inadequate to provide sufficient merchandise to meet sales demand.

Should these or other risks materialize, causing revenues or profits to be lower than projected, Rarities Retailing and "Antiques and Uniques" may fail, causing investors to lose all or most of their investment.

RETURN ON INVESTMENT

Rarities Retailing will be organized as a partnership, with a total partnership capital contribution of $250,000. Investors will provide $200,000 and Ms. Hystyle will contribute $50,000 plus her expertise in the industry.

On an initial investment of $250,000, the percent after-tax cash return on the total investment is:

	Fiscal Year				
	1	2	3	4	5
After-Tax Cash Return on Total Investment	12.0%	6.0%	160.0%	200.0%	240.0%

NOTE: Investors will receive, in addition to their share of the equity, 100% of the depreciation expense for the first five years to shelter their share of the income. This will increase their effective return commensurately.

SAMPLE PROPOSAL III

SYSTEMS SERVICE CORPORATION

FINANCING PROPOSAL

Prepared as of March, 19XX

SYSTEMS SERVICE CORPORATION

TABLE OF CONTENTS

OVERVIEW

Systems Service Corporation (SSC) owns the rights to a computer program which is capable of debugging major computer programs much more efficiently and quickly than any other current method. The program can distinguish between program logic errors and machine malfunctions, and represents a breakthrough in computer software technology.

The program was developed by SSC's founders, Mr. Mike Rochip and Ms. Nan O'Sekund. It has been extensively tested and testimonials to its effectiveness are available. SSC also plans to develop new programs for other applications, all of which represent similar breakthroughs in their respective areas.

The market for SSC's products consists of every company in the world which owns or leases a large-scale computer—one which has a cost exceeding $250,000, including peripheral equipment. There are two major competitors now operating in the market. Each enjoys annual revenues in excess of $10,000,000. But, according to large EDP users' groups, most debugging of large programs is currently done in-house, so SSC does not antici- pate having to take business away from the competition to meet its sales projections.

SSC projects that sales in the first year of operations will be $1,000,000, growing to $9,500,000 by the fifth year. Sales at that level are expected to generate pre-tax profits of $3.7 million in the fifth year.

SSC requires a total initial investment of $550,000, which will generate a pre-tax return on investment of 70% per annum. This magnitude of return is consistent with similar investments in the computer industry.

PROJECT DESCRIPTION

Systems Service Corporation (SSC) owns the rights to a computer program developed by the company's founders, Mr. Mike Rochip and Ms. Nan O'Sekund. The program is capable of debugging large-scale computer programs in a few days, compared to current manual debugging methods which can take months or even years, depending on the scope of the program. SSC's program can debug any program, in any computer language, on any large-scale computer. It can distinguish between program logic errors, system errors and machine malfunctions. It tests and diagnoses any type of software problem.

The program has been developed and extensively tested by Mr. Rochip and Ms. O'Sekund. The five companies on whose equipment the program was tested will provide testimonials upon request. They are also SSC's first paying customers.

SSC will provide the program along with an experienced technical representative to its customers. The work will be done at the customer's site, reducing SSC's initial office needs and overhead expenses.

SSC is also developing new products. The
product which currently is closest to full
development will automatically write computer
programs from English language instructions. The
program has been tested using story problems from
high school math textbooks and has performed
perfectly. The program has a conversational
aspect, in that it asks the user for additional
information needed to develop the program. This
program is expected to be available for license
by the middle of the third year.

Other programs are currently under development, but none are sufficiently developed to have
an impact on the company over its first five years.

MARKET DESCRIPTION

The market for Service Systems Corporation's
(SSC) debugging program consists of every company
in the world which owns or leases a large-scale
computer. A large-scale computer is defined as
one which has an original cost in excess of
$250,000, including peripheral equipment. Com-
panies which have such computers typically employ
an EDP staff of 10 to 15 technical people. SSC
has determined that there are 115,000 large-scale
computer installations in the United States,
including more than 7,500 in this state alone.

SSC plans to provide its customers with
debugging services for up to six major programs
for its basic program rental fee of $25,000. There
will be an additional charge of $5,000 for any
extra program debugged during the course of an
engagement. The technical support for the
debugging services is provided at an average
billing rate of $230 per day, with a minimum of
$5,000 per engagement, covering the first month's
services. The average engagement is expected to
last one month. SSC expects to secure return
engagements from its clients every two to three

years, as they develop new programs.

The size of the market is significant, but is
hard to quantify because such a large portion of
the debugging is currently being done by in-house
staff. The costs of such efforts are tremendous,
since it takes an average of six months for an in-
house staff to completely debug a major program.
This estimate comes from the Association for Bug
Prevention, an affiliate of EDP User's Group, the
largest national organization for computer users,
with over 15,000 member companies.

There are currently two major providers of
contract debugging services, although their
efforts are still manual. These two companies are
"Rid-A-Bug" and "Bug Byters, Inc." Each company
employs approximately 175 technical staff, which
are billed out at $30 per hour, on average. The
annual revenues for each company are over
$10,000,000. The market is considered large
enough that SSC will not have to take customers
from the competition in order to meet its sales
projections, at least for the first five years.

SSC expects to sell 10 service contracts during

the first year, increasing to 20 contracts in the second year, 30 in the third year, and 40 in the fourth and fifth years. SSC technical staff will also be available for contract programming services other than debugging. Revenues from such services, billed on an hourly basis, are expected to exceed program service contract revenues for the first four years of operation.

SSC will also sell its debugging program outright for $100,000 to large users who desire to own the program rather than contract its use. SSC has had indications that several government agencies have an interest in buying the program. No sales of the program are included in the financial projections for SSC.

The market for SSC's new products, especially the program to write programs, is primarily computer manufacturers. In order to make their products more marketable, the manufacturers must make them easier for the layman to operate. SSC's program writer does exactly that. SSC expects to license computer manufacturers to incorporate the program writer into the software for their computers for a royalty of 1% of sales. Total

computer equipment sales in the United States is
approximately $20,000,000,000 annually. SSC
believes its program writer will be applicable to
50% of those sales.

SSC expects to achieve a market penetration of
1% in the first year of sales for the program writer
(year three of SSC's existence). Sales and market
penetration will double in the second year and
double again in the third year, reaching 4%
penetration of the applicable market, and earning
royalties of $4,000,000 in that year.

MARKETING STRATEGY

Systems Service Corporation's (SSC) products are not sold to the public. They will be sold primarily to managers of large EDP systems in major corporations. SSC's marketing strategy is based on the much lower total cost and much faster completion of debugging operations compared to current manual debugging methods. Most manual debugging efforts take several months to complete the same operations SSC can perform in one week.

Most sales will be accomplished by visits to the client's facilities by one of SSC's salespeople. In the beginning, SSC management will handle all sales, with primary responsibility for sales belonging to the Vice President of Marketing, Ms. Meg Abyte. As the company grows, additional salespeople will be added as necessary. Salespeople will be given a 7% commission on the sales they generate, including both the program fee and technical support fees. New product sales will be handled by Ms. Abyte personally until volume justifies additional staff.

In addition to sales calls, SSC will conduct

direct mail campaigns using mailing lists of EDP
managers in companies with large-scale computer
installations. Direct mail will be supplemented
by low key advertisements in computer magazines
and trade journals. The principals in SSC have
many years' experience in the computer industry,
and have numerous contacts among the users and
manufacturers throughout the industry.

SSC's products have an excitement about them
that will allow an extensive public relations
effort, including articles in major mass magazines, such as Time and Newsweek, and in the
business media, such as Forbes and Fortune
magazines, the Wall Street Week television show,
and other media.

CAPITAL REQUIREMENTS

Since Systems Service Corporation (SSC) is a service organization, there are no major capital items required by the company. The investment of $500,000 is needed to cover the salaries of technical and support personnel and to pay back the development costs of the programs owned by SSC.

SSC projects an operating loss in its first year, but expects to be profitable by year two, and will have no further need for investment.

PERSONNEL

Systems Service Corporation (SSC) expects to have a technical staff of 26 by the end of the first year, growing to approximately 60 by the end of the fifth year. SSC expects turnover in its technical staff averaging 10% per year, and expects to be able to use outside employment agencies to handle its employment needs. The market for technical people is tight, but not unmanageable.

There will also be approximately four highly qualified technical people involved in ongoing R & D for SSC's new products. These personnel will be promoted from SSC's technical service staff.

SSC's beginning office staff will consist of one administrative assistant, who will handle billing, payroll, mail and telephones. As the technical staff grows, the office staff will increase to handle the increased billing, payroll and mailings. An office staff will be almost twenty.

Sales personnel will be paid commissions only.

Commissions for the entire sales staff will amount to 10% of sales. Ms. Abyte will be responsible for hiring the sales staff and setting their compensation. Ms. Abyte will receive the difference between the sales commissions and the sales payroll. During the first year, Ms. Abyte, the Vice President of Marketing, will handle all sales calls. One sales person will be added in the second year, and there will be 10 sales people by the end of the fifth year.

MANAGEMENT

SSC's management team consists of the developers of the company's debugging program, Mr. Mike Rochip and Ms. Nan O'Sekund, who will be President and Executive Vice President, respectively, and Ms. Meg Abyte, who will be Vice President of Marketing.

Mr. Rochip has spent 15 years with National Business Machines as a Systems Engineer and troubleshooter. While with NBM, he helped develop the new XAMOS currently used on all NBM equipment. He is a graduate of the Sam Houston Institute of Technology in Texas.

Ms. O'Sekund has worked for the last eight years for Arkansas Instruments, developing operating systems for AI computers. Prior to that she was employed in her native Ireland by the Irish subsidiary of National Business Machines.

Ms. Abyte has served for 10 years in the Large System Marketing Division of Data Control Corporation, the last two as Manager of Corporate Sales. In her duties with DCC, Ms. Abyte managed a staff of more than one hundred and enjoyed excellent customer relations. She personally knows the key managers at many of SSC's potential customers. DCC has stated that there is no conflict of interest arising from Ms. Abyte's new duties with SSC.

The management capabilities of the three principals of SSC are such that SSC will rank among the best managed companies in the industry.

SYSTEMS SERVICE CORPORATION
PROJECTED STATEMENTS OF PROFIT AND LOSS
FIRST FIVE YEARS
(In Thousands)

	FISCAL YEAR				
	First	Second	Third	Fourth	Fifth
Revenues:					
Software Sales	$250	$500	$1,750	$3,000	$5,000
Consulting Fees	750	1810	2,750	3,600	4,500
Total Revenues	$1,000	$2,310	$4,500	$6,600	$9,500
Expenses					
Technical Salaries	$381	$930	$1,400	$1,900	$2,400
Sales Commissions	100	231	450	660	950
Overhead Salaries	120	190	310	500	700
R&D Salaries	144	216	240	265	290
Payroll Taxes &					
Fringe Benefits	103	235	300	400	520
Rent	12	22	75	100	150
Travel & Entertainment	30	52	100	180	250
Office Expenses	18	40	60	75	100
Recruiting Expenses	270	120	245	190	260
Depreciation &					
Leasehold Imp.	6	11	20	30	50
Other	24	42	70	100	125
Total Expenses	$1,208	$2,089	$3,270	$4,400	$5,795
Profit (Loss) Before					
Income Taxes	$(208)	$221	$1,230	$2,200	$3,705

SYSTEMS SERVICE CORPORATION
PROJECTED STATEMENT OF PROFIT AND LOSS
FIRST YEAR
(In Thousands)

	APR	MAY	JUN	JUL	AUG	SEP	OCT	NOV	DEC	JAN	FEB	MAR	TOTAL
Revenues													
Software Sales	—	—	$25	—	—	$50	—	—	—	$75	—	$100	$250
Consulting Fees	—	$15	25	$30	$50	50	$70	$80	$70	100	$130	130	750
Total Revenues	—	$15	$50	$30	$50	$100	$70	$80	$70	$175	$130	$230	$1,000
Expenses													
Technical Salaries	$3	$6	$12	$15	$25	$25	$35	$40	$40	$50	$65	$65	$381
Sales Commisions	—	2	5	3	5	10	7	8	7	17	13	23	100
Overhead Salaries	10	10	10	10	10	10	10	10	10	10	10	10	120
R&D Salaries	12	12	12	12	12	12	12	12	12	12	12	12	144
Payroll Taxes & Fringe Benefits	3	4	5	5	7	8	9	10	10	13	13	16	103
Rent	1	1	1	1	1	1	1	1	1	1	1	1	12
Travel & Entertainment	2	4	3	3	3	3	3	—	—	4	3	2	30
Office Expense	1	2	1	2	1	2	1	2	1	2	1	2	18
Recruiting Expense	45	9	27	9	36	—	36	18	—	36	54	—	270
Depreciation & Leasehold Imp	—	1	—	1	—	1	—	1	—	1	—	1	6
Other	2	2	2	2	2	2	2	2	2	2	2	2	24
Total Expenses	$79	$53	$78	$63	$102	$74	$116	$104	$83	$148	$174	$134	$1,208
Profit (Loss) Before Income Taxes	$(79)	$(38)	$(28)	$(33)	$(52)	$26	$(46)	$(24)	$(13)	$27	$(44)	$96	$(208)

SYSTEMS SERVICE CORPORATION
PROJECTED STATEMENT OF PROFIT AND LOSS
SECOND YEAR
(In Thousands)

	APR	MAY	JUN	JUL	AUG	SEP	OCT	NOV	DEC	JAN	FEB	MAR	TOTAL
Revenues													
Software Sales	$25	$50	$50	$25	—	$25	$50	—	—	$100	$100	$75	$500
Consulting Fees	130	150	150	150	150	150	150	150	100	170	180	180	1,810
Total Revenues	$155	$200	$200	$175	$150	$175	$200	$150	$100	$270	$280	$255	$2,310
Expenses													
Technical Salaries	$65	$75	$75	$75	$75	$75	$75	$75	$75	$85	$90	$90	$930
Sales Commisions	15	20	20	18	15	17	20	15	10	27	28	26	231
Overhead Salaries	14	14	14	15	15	16	17	17	17	17	17	17	190
R&D Salaries	18	18	18	18	18	18	18	18	18	18	18	18	216
Payroll Taxes & Fringe Benefits	17	19	19	19	18	19	19	19	18	22	23	23	235
Rent	1	1	2	2	2	2	2	2	2	2	2	2	22
Travel & Entertainment	4	5	5	5	4	4	4	4	2	5	5	5	52
Office Expense	2	3	3	4	3	4	3	4	2	4	3	4	40
Recruiting Expense	18	18	—	10	—	11	—	9	—	27	18	9	120
Depreciation & Leasehold Imp	—	1	1	1	1	1	1	1	1	1	1	1	11
Other	3	4	3	4	3	4	3	4	3	4	3	4	42
Total Expenses	$157	$178	$160	$171	$154	$171	$162	$168	$149	$212	$208	$199	$2089
Profit (Loss) Before Income Taxes	$(2)	$22	$40	$4	$(4)	$4	$38	$(18)	$(49)	$58	$72	$56	$221

SYSTEMS SERVICE CORPORATION

PROJECTED STATEMENTS OF PROFIT AND LOSS

ASSUMPTIONS

Revenues:

Software Sales:

SSC's Debugging Program will be marketed to every company with a large-scale computer installation.   There   are   currently   100,000   such installations in the country, including 2,000 in this state alone. SSC expects to concentrate on the in-state market exclusively during the first five years, with market penetration of 0.5% in the first year, 1.0% in the second year, 1.5% in the third year, and 2.0% in the fourth and fifth years. This market penetration will result in sales of Debugging Program contracts in the first five years of 10,20,30,40 and 40, respectively, at $25,000 per contract.

Program Writing Software will be marketed to computer manufacturers, beginning in the third year of operation. SSC will license the Program Writer to manufacturers for a fee of 1% of the sales price of the equipment. Computer equipment sales are currently in excess of $20,000,000,000 per year in the United States, with 50% being computers and 50% being peripheral equipment, not applicable to Program Writer license. Based on those figures, the maximum market for the Program Writer is $100,000,000 (1% of 50% of $20,000,000,000). SSC expects to realize a market penetration of 1% during the first year the program is offered, doubling to 2% in the second year of offering and doubling again to 4% in the third year. Assuming no growth in the market for computer equipment, the above will produce revenues of $1,000,000, $2,000,000, and $4,000,000, in the third, fourth and fifth years of operation, respectively.

Consulting Fees:

Consulting fees arise from the rental of SSC's technical people by other companies' EDP Departments for contract programming. In addition, there are $5,000 in consulting fees with each sale of the Debugging Program, representing the one month minimum length of the contract. SSC's technical personnel are billed at twice their salary, and their time is expected to be fully utilized by client work. By the end of year one, SSC expects to have 26 technical staff, increasing to 33 at the end of year two, 45 in year three, 51 in year four and 59 at the end if year five. Billing rates will average $5,000 per month in year one, $5,500 per month in year two, $6,000 in year three, $6,700 per month in year four and $7,300 per month in year five. Technical staff increases will be spread throughout the year.

In year one, Consulting Fees are projected to be $750,000, of which $50,000 result from Debugging Program contract sales. Fees in year one start out slowly, as contracts are signed and technical people are hired. In the month of December, there is a slight decrease due to the holiday season. In year two, Consulting Fees increase to $1,810,000, primarily because there are 26 technical staff available for the entire year. Billing rates increase 10% and Consulting Fees from Debugging Program contracts are $110,000 (20 sales at $5,500). In year three, Consulting Fees increase to $2,750,000, of which $180,000 is due to Debugging Program contracts. Billing rates increase 10%. In year four, Consulting Fees grow to $3,600,000 ($268,000 from sales of the Debugging Program). Billing rates increase 10%. In the fifth year, Consulting Fees reach $4,500,000

($292,000 from Debugging Program contracts), with a technical staff of over 50. Billing rates increase 10%.

Expenses:

Technical Salaries are based on average salaries for trained programmers, of $30,000 in the first year, $33,000 in the second year, $36,000 in the third year, $40,000 in the fourth year, and $44,000 in the fifth year. Employment at the end of each of those years is expected to be 26, 33, 45, 51 and 59, respectively. New hires will be spread out over the year, after year two, with each averaging one-half year's employment in their first year with SSC.

Sales Commissions will be 10% of Total Revenues. No draws or Sales Salaries will be paid. The number of sales people is expected to reach 10 by the end of year five.

Overhead Salaries include Mr. Rochip, Ms. O'Sekund and the office staff. The office staff at the end of each of the five years is expected to be 1, 4, 10, 13 and 18. Average office salaries for each of the years are projected at $12,000,

$15,000, $16,000, $18,000 and $20,000. New hires
are assumed to be added at mid-year.

R & D Salaries consist of the salaries of
persons involved in developing the program-
writing software during the first two years. It
is projected that there will be four technicians
at an average salary of $36,000 in the first year,
and 6 technicians at an average of $36,000 in the
second year. In years three through five, it is
assumed that the six technicians will continue to
work, while their salaries increase 10% per year.

Payroll Taxes and Fringe Benefits include FICA
taxes, Unemployment taxes, Workman's Compensation
taxes and Health Insurance. These costs are
projected to be 15% of salaries and commissions
for years one and two, dropping to 12% of salaries
and commissions in years three through five, as
individual salaries exceed the cutoff levels for
the various employment taxes.

Rent in the first year assumes an office of
1,000 square feet, at an annual rental of $12 per
square foot. In year two, as the office staff
grows, the office size is doubled to 2,000 square

feet, with the rent remaining at $12. In the third year, new offices in more exclusive quarters increase the space to 4,000 square feet, at an annual rental rate of just under $20 per square foot. In the fourth and fifth years, with sales seminars held on the premises and the growing office and marketing staff needs, the square footage increases to 5,000 and 6,000, respectively, while the annual rental rate increases to $20 and $25.

Travel and Entertainment for the marketing and executive staffs increases each year to reflect inflation, increased staff sizes, and the costs associated with the sales seminars held in years four and five.

Office Expense includes Office Equipment Rentals, Postage (other than direct mail), Printing, Training Materials, Telephone, Coffee and Coke Machines, etc. These costs increase each year, reflecting the larger offices and staff.

Recruiting Expense results from the extremely tight market and high salaries for trained technical people. Employment agencies will be heavily utilized. Their average commission rate is 30% of the first year's salary of the new hire, which, when applied to the average salaries of technical people, by year, produces average commission of $9,000 per new hire in the first year, growing to $10,000, $11,000, $12,000 and $13,000 in the next four years, respectively. The number of new hires for technical people include new positions, plus 10% turnover in existing positions. Turnover increases to 20% in years three through five. Thus the number of new hires in the technical staff will be: In year one—30 (including 4 R&D); Year two—12 (including 2 R&D and 3 turnover); Year three—20 (including 8 turnover); Year four—14 (including 8 turnover); and Year five—18 (including 10 turnover). In addition, some of the office staff, but not all, will be hired through employment agencies. In year one, we expect to hire through contacts, and the same in year two. In year three, we expect to hire 6 staff through agencies and 3 more in year four. In year five we expect to use agencies for 5 office staff. Average employment fees for office staff are projected to be $4,000 in years three and four, and $5,000 in year five.

Depreciation and Leasehold Improvements consists of office furnishings only, all of which has
a three year life.   SSC uses straight line
depreciation and takes a full year's depreciation
in the first year of use.   Capital additions
include $18,000 of office furniture in the first
year, $15,000 in the second year, $27,000 in the
third year, $48,000 in the fourth year and $75,000
in the fifth year.

Other expense includes Audit expense, which is
projected to be, by year, $15,000, $25,000,
$30,000, $50,000 and $60,000. Other expense also
includes the cost of direct mail. The remainder
of Other expense consists of minor miscellaneous
items, none of which exceed $25,000 in any year.

SYSTEMS SERVICE CORPORATION
STATEMENT OF PROJECTED CASH REQUIREMENTS
FIRST FIVE YEARS
(In Thousands)

	FISCAL YEAR				
	First	Second	Third	Fourth	Fifth
Sources of Cash					
Profit (Loss) from					
Operations	$(208)	$221	$1,230	$2,200	$3,705
Add: Depreciation	6	11	20	30	50
Timing Adjustments					
for Expenses	23	24	24	16	30
Deduct: Timing Adj.					
for Revenue	(130)	(50)	(595)	(585)	(1,090)
Cash Flow from					
Operations	$(309)	$206	$679	$1,661	$2,695
Purchase of Stock					
by Founders	50	—	—	—	—
Total Sources of Cash	$(259)	$206	$679	$1,661	$2,695
Uses of Cash					
Capital Additions	$18	$15	$27	$48	$75
Repayment of Loans	50	150	—	—	—
Purchase of Program Rights	50	100	150	200	200
Total Uses of Cash	$118	$265	$177	$248	$275
Net Cash Requirements	$(377)	$(59)	$502	$1,413	$2,420
Cumulative Cash					
Requirements	$(377)	$(436)	$66	$1,479	$3,899

SYSTEMS SERVICE CORPORATION

STATEMENT OF PROJECTED CASH REQUIREMENTS

FIRST YEAR

(In Thousands)

	APR	MAY	JUN	JUL	AUG	SEP	OCT	NOV	DEC	JAN	FEB	MAR	TOTAL
Sources of Cash													
Profit (Loss) Before Taxes	$(79)	$(38)	$(28)	$(33)	$(52)	$26	$(46)	$(24)	$(13)	$27	$(44)	$96	$(208)
Add: Depreciation	–	1	–	1	–	1	–	1	–	1	–	1	6
Timing Adjusrment for Expenses	54	(32)	17	(17)	28	(16)	18	(19)	(19)	44	16	(51)	23
Deduct: Timing Adj. for Revenues	–	(15)	(10)	(5)	(20)	–	(20)	(10)	10	(30)	(30)	–	(130)
Cash Flow from Operations	$(25)	$(84)	$(21)	$(54)	$(44)	$11	$(48)	$(52)	$(22)	$42	$(58)	$46	$(309)
Purchase of Stock by Founders	50	–	–	–	–	–	–	–	–	–	–	–	50
Total Sources of Cash	$25	$(84)	$(21)	$(54)	$(44)	$11	$(48)	$(52)	$(22)	$42	$(58)	$46	$(259)
Uses of Cash													
Capital Additions	$18	–	–	–	–	–	–	–	–	–	–	–	$18
Repayment of Loans for Officers	50	–	–	–	–	–	–	–	–	–	–	–	50
Purchase of Program Rights	–	–	$5	–	–	$10	–	–	–	$15	–	$20	50
Total Uses of Cash	$68	–	$5	–	–	$10	–	–	–	$15	–	$20	$118
Net Cash Requirements	$(43)	$(84)	$(26)	$(54)	$(44)	$1	$(48)	$(52)	$(22)	$27	$(58)	$26	$(377)
Cumulative Cash Requirements	$(43)	$(127)	$(153)	$(207)	$(251)	$(250)	$(298)	$(350)	$(372)	$(345)	$(403)	$(377)	

SYSTEMS SERVICE CORPORATION
STATEMENT OF PROJECTED CASH REQUIREMENTS
SECOND YEAR
(In Thousands)

	APR	MAY	JUN	JUL	AUG	SEP	OCT	NOV	DEC	JAN	FEB	MAR	TOTAL
Sources of Cash													
Profit (Loss) Before Taxes	$(2)	$22	$40	$4	$(4)	$4	$38	$(18)	$(49)	$58	$72	$56	$221
Add: Depreciation	–	1	1	1	1	1	1	1	1	1	1	1	11
Timing Adjusrment for Expenses	22	5	(18)	12	(14)	14	(13)	11	(14)	36	(10)	(7)	24
Deduct: Timing Adj. for Revenues	–	(20)	–	–	–	–	–	–	50	(70)	(10)	–	(50)
Cash Flow from Operations	$20	$8	$23	$17	$(17)	$19	$26	$(6)	$(12)	$25	$53	$50	$206
Uses of Cash													
Capital Additions	–	–	$15	–	–	–	–	–	–	–	–	–	$15
Repayment of Loans for Officers	–	–	–	–	–	–	–	–	–	–	–	$150	150
Purchase of Program Rights	$5	$10	10	$5	–	$5	$10	–	–	$20	$20	15	100
Total Uses of Cash	$5	$10	$25	$5	–	$5	$10	–	–	$20	$20	$165	$265
Net Cash Requirements	$15	$(2)	$(2)	$12	$(17)	$14	$16	$(6)	$(12)	$5	$33	$(115)	$(59)
Cumulative Cash Requirements	$(362)	$(364)	$(366)	$(354)	$(371)	$(357)	$(341)	$(347)	$(359)	$(354)	$(321)	$(436)	

SYSTEMS SERVICE CORPORATION

STATEMENT OF PROJECTED CASH REQUIREMENTS

ASSUMPTIONS

Timing Adjustments for Revenues:

Debugging Program Sales are received in the month in which they are recorded.

Royalties from new programs will be received semiannually, beginning in the third year. Half the royalties recorded as sales on the Statements of Profit and Loss in the third fourth and fifth years, will not be received until the following year.

Consulting Fees are received in the month following the month in which they are earned, a one-month lag in receipts. In the third, fourth and fifth years, the lag is assumed to represent 10% of the year's volume, consistent with the first two years.

Timing Adjustments for Expenses consists of payments for expenses other than payroll and Depreciation occurring in the month following the month they are incurred on the Statements of Profit and Loss, a one-month lag in payments. In years three, four and five, the expense lag is assumed at one twelfth of the applicable yearly expense totals.

Purchase of Stock by Founders represents the payment by Mr. Rochip and Ms. O'Sekund for the purchase of 500,000 shares of SSC stock at 10 cents per share.

Capital Additions are for office furniture and equipment.

Repayment of Loans is the reimbursement of Mr. Rochip and Ms. O'Sekund for the expenses and payroll costs incurred in the development of the Debugging Program. These expenses amount to $200,000. Payment will be made in two installments: $50,000 upon receiving financing, and the remaining $150,000 at the end of the first year in which the company shows a profit.

Purchase of Program Rights is the purchase of the rights to the Debugging Program developed by Mr. Rochip and Ms. O'Sekund. The purchase terms call for the payment of 20% of the user fees for the Debugging Program for the first five years.

Payments occur in the same month that sales and
cash receipts are recorded. At the end of five
years, SSC owns all rights to the program, and all
future program developed will belong to SSC from
the beginning.

SYSTEMS SERVICE CORPORATION
PROJECTED BALANCE SHEETS
FIRST FIVE YEARS
(In Thousands)

ASSETS	Beginning Balance	End of year First	Second	Third	Fourth	Fifth
Current Assets						
Cash	$500	$123	$64	$114	$255	$497
Accounts Receivable	—	130	180	775	1,360	2,450
Total Current Assets	$500	$253	$244	$889	$1,615	$2,947
Furniture & Fixtures		$18	$33	$42	$75	$123
Less: Accum. Deprec.		6	17	19	34	57
Net Furn. & Fixtures		12	16	23	41	66
Other Assets:						
Program Rights		$50	$150	$300	$500	$700
Program Costs	$200	200	200	200	200	200
Total Assets	$700	$515	$610	$1,412	$2,356	$3,913
Liabilities & Stockholders' Equity						
Current Liabilities:						
Accounts Payable	—	$23	$47	$71	$87	$117
Loans Payable	$200	150	—	—	—	—
Total Current Libilities	$200	$173	$47	$71	$87	$117
Stockholders' Equity						
Capital Stock Par Value (10¢)	$50	$100	$100	$100	$100	$100
Capital In Excess of Par Value	450	450	450	450	450	450
Retained Earnings	—	(208)	13	1,243	3,443	7,148
Less: Dividends Paid	—	—	—	(452)	(1,724)	(3,902)
Total Equity	$500	$342	$563	$1,341	$2,269	$3,796
Total Liabilities and Stockholders' Equity	$700	$515	$610	$1,412	$2,356	$3,913

SYSTEMS SERVICE CORPORATION

PROJECTED BALANCE SHEET

ASSUMPTIONS

Cash beginning balance is comprised of the $500,000 raised from investors. Subsequent increases and decreases in Cash reflect activity from the Projected Statements of Cash Requirements, plus Dividends Paid.

Accounts Receivable in the first two years consist of the Consulting Fees recorded in the last month of the fiscal year. In the third and subsequent years, Accounts Receivable consists of The last month's Consulting Fees (10% of annual volume) plus one-half of the year's program royalties, which are received semiannually. Debugging Program user fees are paid as recorded, and no Accounts Receivable arise therefrom.

Furniture and Fixtures and **Depreciation** refer to office furniture and equipment, all of which has a three year life. Fully depreciated assets are removed from the accounts along with the related accumulated depreciation.

Other Assets consist of intangible assets relating to the Debugging Program. Program Rights are purchased with 20% of the program user fees paid to SSC during the first five years. Program Costs are the expenses incurred in developing the program, which are repaid to the founders according to the agreements. The beginning balance in Program Costs is the amount of the Loan Payable for the expenses incurred. Program Rights amounts arise as payments are made. Program Rights and Program Costs will be depreciated over five years, beginning in the sixth year, after all payments have been made.

Accounts Payable is obtained from the Projected Statements of Cash Requirements, representing the one-month lag in paying expenses other than payroll and depreciation.

Loans Payable represents the Program Costs discussed above. Changes in the account come from payments shown on the Statements of Cash Requirements.

Capital Stock—Par Value and **Capital In Excess of Par Value** represent the purchase of 500,000

shares of Capital Stock at 10 cents per share
($50,000) and the payment of an additional
$450,000 by outside investors. The addition in
the first year reflects the purchase of 500,000
shares at 10 cents per share by the founders,
immediately after the company is formed.

Retained Earnings increase or decrease by the
amount of PreTax Income shown on the Projected
Statements of Profit or Loss. Income Taxes are
ignored because, as an S Corporation, SSC passes
revenues and expenses through to its shareholders.

Dividends Paid is the cumulative amount of
dividends paid to shareholders. SSC's dividend
policy is to pay out 90% of the cash flow in each
year in which there is a positive cash flow.
Dividends are not shown on the Statements of Cash
Requirements.

CONFLICTS OF INTEREST, FEES AND RISKS

SSC's founders, Mr. Rochip and Ms. O'Sekund, have incurred costs in the development of the debugging program in the amount of $200,000. The company will repay the founders for those costs in two installments: $50,000 upon formation of the company, and $150,000 at the end of the first year in which the company shows a profit, on the accrual basis, without consideration of the effects of the payment to the founders. This is projected to occur in the second year. No interest will accrue on this amount.

In addition, the founders have agreed to sell the rights to the debugging program to the company for an amount equal to 20% of the program service fees received by the company for the rental of the program during the first five years. Payments under this program are projected to total $700,000, on revenues of $3,500,000 over the five years.

The founders will purchase 50% of the capital stock of SSC (500,000 shares at 10 cents per share) immediately following the formation of the company.

Mr. Rochip and Ms. O'Sekund, as President and Vice President, respectively, will each receive salaries of $54,000 in the first year, $75,000 in the second year, $100,000 in the third year, $150,000 in the fourth year, and $200,000 in the fifth year. The salary increases will be approved each year by the Board of Directors and will be contingent on the company meeting certain speci- fied revenue and profit goals. In addition, Mr. Rochip and Ms. O'Sekund together will receive 50% of the cash dividends paid.

Sales commissions will be 10% of revenues, both consulting fees and program sales. Ms. Abyte will receive all sales commissions not paid to her sales staff.   During the first year, Ms. Abyte will handle all sales personally and will receive all sales commissions, expected to total $100,000. By the fifth year, Ms. Abyte expects to have a sales force of 10 salespeople, each earning approxi- mately $65,000, with Ms. Abyte receiving the remainder of the sales commissions, an amount projected to be $300,000.

The risks associated with an investment in Systems Service Corporation are common to investments in similar high-technology companies. Other companies may independently develop the same program capabilities, which could severely erode SSC's sales. In addition, as new computer technology evolves, SSC's proprietary software may become obsolete.

Should these, or any other, problems arise causing SSC's revenues or profits to be below projections, or expenses to exceed projections, SSC could easily fail, resulting in the loss of all or substantially all the monies invested in SSC.

RETURN ON INVESTMENT

Systems Service Corporation (SSC) will be organized as an S Corporation, so that expenses and revenues are passed through to the investors to be recognized on their individual tax returns.

SSC requires an investment of $500,000 from outside investors, which will entitle the investors to 50% of the equity of the company. The founders, Mr. Rochip and Ms, O'Sekund, will invest $50,000 plus their expertise in the industry for the remaining 50% of the stock.

The dividend policy of the company will be to pay out 90% of the cash flow for the year, after the second year. The payout in the third year will be $452,000; in the fourth year, $1,330,000; and in the fifth year, $2,178,000. Based on a maximum individual tax rate of 28%, and using the projections found in the earlier section, an investor in SSC would expect to realize the returns shown below.

($ in Thousands)

	Fiscal Year				
	1	2	3	4	5
50% of PreTax Income	($104)	$110	$615	$1,100	$1,852
Taxes Due @ 28%	N/A	$2*	$172	$308	$519
50% of Dividends Paid	$0	$0	$226	$665	$1,089
Net AfterTax Cash	$0	($2)	$54	$357	$570
% Cash Return	0%	(.4%)	10.8%	71.4%	114.0%

*NOTE: Second Year earnings are offset by First Year loss.

There is also the possibility that the company will have a public offering of its stock after the fifth year. PreTax earnings are projected to be $3,705,000 in the fifth year. If those earnings are capitalized at 10 times (not unreasonable, given the rapid growth in earnings experienced by the company), then the company's stock is worth more than $37,000,000. The investors' share of the company would be worth approximately $18,500,000.